nine by nine

nine by nine

9-Patch Quilts, 9 Ways

CYNDI HERSHEY

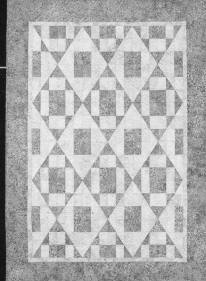

Martingale®
& COMPANY

Nine by Nine: 9-Patch Quilts, 9 Ways
© 2007 by Cyndi Hershey

That Patchwork Place® is an imprint of
Martingale & Company®.

Martingale & Company
20205 144th Ave. NE
Woodinville, WA 98072-8478 USA
www.martingale-pub.com

Credits
President & CEO: Tom Wierzbicki
Publisher: Jane Hamada
Editorial Director: Mary V. Green
Managing Editor: Tina Cook
Developmental Editor: Karen Costello Soltys
Technical Editor: Laurie Baker
Copy Editor: Sheila Chapman Ryan
Design Director: Stan Green
Assistant Design Director: Regina Girard
Illustrator: Robin Strobel
Cover Designer: Stan Green
Text Designer: Patricia Field
Photographer: Brent Kane

Mission Statement
Dedicated to providing quality products
and service to inspire creativity.

Printed in China
12 11 10 09 08 07   8 7 6 5 4 3 2 1

Library of Congress Cataloging-in-Publication Data
Library of Congress Control Number: 2007028336

ISBN: 978-1-56477-736-2

Dedication

To the power of friendship!
This book would not have been possible
if not for the loving support and help
that I received from my friends.
Thanks to all of you for
always being there.

Acknowledgments

Many thanks to Doris Adomsky for allowing me to use her "Perkiomen Valley Nine Patch" quilt (page 56). In addition, the many hours she spent piecing and binding quilts are much appreciated. Thank you again.

Thank you to Mary Covey, Kim Pope, Pat Burns, and Angela Baker for your incredible machine quilting.

Thank you to my binding buddies: Marcy McGuire, Pat Marburger, Kim Pope, and Pamela Wojtusik. You provided the finishing touches!

To all my friends at Martingale, your expertise and support are priceless.

Thanks to P&B Textiles for many of the fabrics used to make these quilts. Also, thanks to Julie Scribner, Lynn Boyer, Sharon Johnson, Tommie Parker, and Lianne Buhs for all of your help and support.

And to Jim. Thank you for putting up with a crazy quilter this past year!

Contents

What Is a Nine Patch?

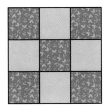 

Nine Patch blocks

Nine Patch is one of the most-used terms in quilting! Did you know that it refers to the name of both a particular quilt block as well as an entire category of blocks? I love the simple Nine Patch block for its strong graphic lines. It always appeals to me, whether it is used as the sole design of a quilt or if it is combined with other blocks or elements. The Nine Patch block can stand alone or be used as the foundation for such familiar quilt patterns as the Single Irish Chain or Double Irish Chain.

When a quilt uses Nine Patch blocks set alternately with another block, the Nine Patch blocks form a simple but strong chain that frames the alternate blocks. These alternate blocks can be as simple as a square of an interesting fabric, or they can feature a beautiful quilting design or intricate appliquéd motif.

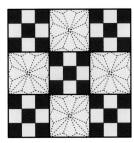

Nine Patch blocks set with
printed-fabric squares

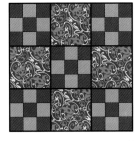

Nine Patch blocks set with
plain, quilted squares

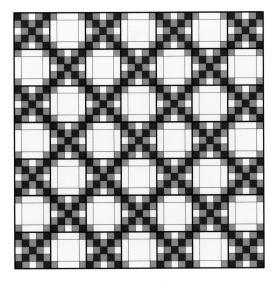

Double Irish Chain

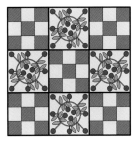

Nine Patch blocks set
with appliqué blocks

The nine-patch *category* of blocks refers to blocks that have seams that divide them equally into nine sections, commonly called units. There are two seams that run in both vertical and horizontal directions, forming an even grid. These nine units can then be divided into smaller pieces that could possibly use several different shapes.

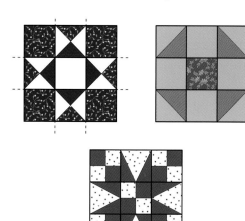

Combining different Nine Patch blocks can be the basis for some wonderful quilt designs! When you sew blocks together that share the same basic grid structure, it adds visual continuity to a pieced quilt. You can see in the following examples how all the major seam lines connect from block to block to create a design that flows smoothly in all directions across the quilt.

Fifty-Four Forty or Fight and Friendship Star

Contrary Wife and Basic Split Nine Patch

One block that's a good candidate for combining with the Nine Patch block is the Snowball block. You can use any size of triangle in the Snowball-block corners, but when based on the same grid as the Nine Patch block, the blocks combine effortlessly to create a perfect union.

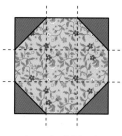

Snowball block

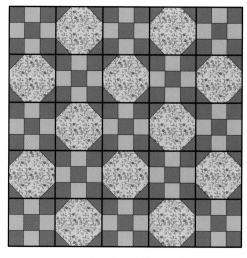

Nine Patch and Snowball

Nine Patch blocks are not limited to placement within the body of a quilt. This book shows you nine different ways to incorporate the concept of a Nine Patch block into various areas within a quilt.

1. Arrange basic Nine Patch blocks in simple settings in "Nearly Neutral" (page 24) and "Posy Patch" (page 28).

2. Look for Nine Patch blocks used in the sashing and/or borders of "Sky Gems" (page 32) and "Peaceful Retreat" (page 36).

3. Set Nine Patch blocks straight and on point for the multiple borders of "Nine Patch Medallion" (page 40).

4. Elongate the basic Nine Patch block in "Some Like It Hot" (page 48).

5. Create Split Nine Patch blocks for "Diamonz" (page 52) and "Perkiomen Valley Nine Patch" (page 56).

6. Combine Nine Patch blocks with nine-patch units in "Winter Blues" (page 60) and "Nine by Nine by Nine" (page 65).

7. Combine a variety of blocks in a double nine-patch setting in "Sudoku Sampler" (page 70).

8. Place nine-patch units in the center of a block in "Picnic Bouquet" (page 80) and "Nine Patch Garden" (page 85).

9. Use a nine-patch design as a quilting design in "Metro Runner" (page 92).

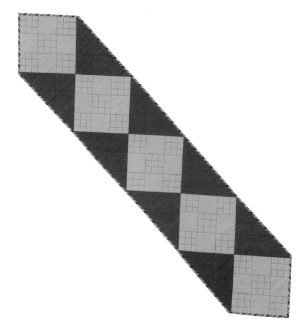

In addition to following the specific instructions for these quilt projects, I hope that you will also feel free to mix and match different elements to make your own unique quilts! You can combine parts of one project with those of another to make totally new designs. When you consider all the options, I'm sure that your ideas will start to flow!

Getting Started

Please read through the general information that follows. Being well prepared before you begin a new project will help ensure that each step of the process will go as smoothly as possible and give you the best results. If you would like more detailed information on any of these topics, I recommend *Your First Book (or it should be!)* by Carol Doak (That Patchwork Place, 1997).

Time to Choose Fabric

Once you've decided to make a project, the first thing that you think about is choosing the fabric. This is great fun for some people and a bit nerve-racking for others! Where do you start? You can use the photos of the sample quilts to give you some ideas, and you can always find helpful and enthusiastic assistance from the staff of your local quilt shop. Show staff members your design or tell them your ideas and they will be able to guide you in selecting fabrics for a truly successful quilt.

Color

I find that many times we are told to concentrate on *color* when choosing fabrics for quilts. While color is certainly something that you will consider, also look carefully at the *values* of the fabrics in the sample quilts.

Value refers to how light or dark a fabric is relative to what is next to it in the design. Value is part of what creates contrast. Low contrast is what causes a design to appear quite soft and delicate while high contrast creates a strong and graphic design. You can see in the three examples below that even though the colors and prints of the fabrics in each quilt differ, the placement of the values remains the same. Using this simple value-placement recipe will help give you the same overall look of the project quilts even though your colors and fabrics will be different.

If you're comfortable branching out, feel free to play with fabrics to your heart's content! When you are making a quilt for yourself, it is easy to think about a color scheme that you may enjoy using in your home now. However, try to avoid "over matching" colors by selecting fabrics for your new quilt that repeat colors that you have used many times before in the room where it will be displayed. Usually, if there is a significant amount of a particular color already in a room, it's more interesting to complement it with other, fresher colors.

Content and Care

The primary type of fabric sold by quilt shops is 100% cotton. Quilters prefer cotton for its stability and ability to hold a pressed edge or seam. It is also easy to quilt by hand or machine.

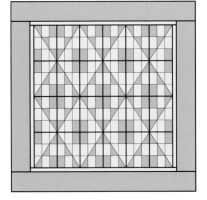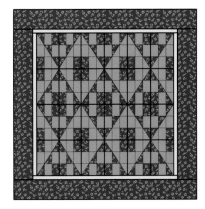

Even though the colors and prints differ, the placement of the light and dark values remains the same in these three examples.

Whether or not you choose to prewash your fabrics is a personal preference. Some quilters prefer the crispness of unwashed fabric. Others prefer to wash and dry the fabrics before cutting, eliminating the risk of any slight shrinkage that may occur when the completed quilt is washed. If you do decide to wash your fabric, use plenty of cool water and a small amount of gentle soap such as Orvus. To maintain the clarity of their color, dry your fabrics in the dryer using very low heat or hang fabrics to dry.

Grain Line

The structure of a fabric is the grain. The grain refers to both the horizontal and vertical threads. The horizontal threads (weft) are commonly referred to as the "crosswise grain." They run across the width of the fabric, perpendicular to the selvages. If you pull a piece of fabric across the width, you will see that there is some amount of stretch. In small pieces, that stretch is generally not noticeable. In large or long pieces, such as borders, it may cause a problem.

The vertical threads (warp) are commonly referred to as the "lengthwise grain." They run parallel to the selvages. If you pull a piece of fabric along the length, you will find that there is no stretch at all. This is the reason that I have instructed you to cut any continuous outer borders for the quilts in this book along the lengthwise grain. Your quilt won't stretch and will retain its original shape.

The diagonal intersecting the two grain lines is called the bias. It has the most amount of stretch. Pieces cut on the bias should never be used on the quilt's outer edges if at all possible.

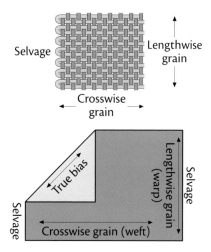

Selvage — Lengthwise grain

Crosswise grain

True bias — Lengthwise grain (warp) — Selvage

Selvage

Crosswise grain (weft)

Basic Supplies

Iron. You don't need a fancy or expensive iron. However, your iron should maintain a consistent *hot* temperature.

Marking tools. For tracing around plastic templates, a fine-point mechanical pencil is sufficient in most cases. You can also use the pencil for lightly marking quilting lines on your completed quilt top. I also like to use a Hera marker for marking fabric. This is a very basic tool that marks the fabric by creating fine creases that are clearly visible on most fabrics. If you make a mistake or change your mind, you can dampen the fabric, press it, and the lines disappear!

Rotary-cutting equipment. This equipment is invaluable to cut the fabrics for your quilt. You will need either a 45-mm or 60-mm rotary cutter, a rotary-cutting mat at least 18" x 24", and several clear plastic rulers. My favorite rulers are a 6" x 12" rectangle, an 8½" x 24" rectangle, an 8" x 8" square, and a 15" x 15" square.

Pins. Silk pins with flat heads or *tiny* glass heads are ideal for pinning two layers of fabric together when preparing to sew a seam. Silk pins are longer than regular dressmaking pins and have a smooth, fine shank. They will cause the least amount of distortion along a seam line, which is a big help when machine piecing.

Scissors. I use a pair of small embroidery scissors for trimming threads and clipping bits of fabric. A pair of dressmaker's shears is also invaluable for cutting larger pieces of fabric.

Sewing machine. If you have not had your sewing machine serviced in quite some time, do it now! We expect a lot from our machines and they work much better when they have regular checkups. So do I! Basic sewing-machine maintenance is easy to do yourself and should be done on a regular basis. However, take your machine to a professional once a year for a thorough cleaning and any necessary adjustments.

Sewing-machine needles. Replace your sewing-machine needle frequently. A general guideline is to replace the needle at the beginning of every new project. It is important to use the proper size and type of needle for your fabric. For piecing on cotton fabrics, a size 70/10 or 80/12 universal or quilting needle is a good choice.

Sewing thread. I prefer to use a good-quality, 50-weight cotton sewing thread to piece my quilts. When sewing on a natural-fiber fabric such as cotton, I use a natural-fiber thread so that the stitches integrate evenly into the fabric along the seam lines.

Template plastic. "Nine Patch Garden" is the only project in this book that requires the use of template plastic. Template plastic is a heavy but translucent plastic sold in sheets at your local quilt shop. It is easy to mark and you can cut it with paper scissors.

Rotary-Cutting Techniques

You will notice that you are asked to cut many strips for the quilts in this book. Cut all strips *across the width of the fabric unless indicated otherwise,* using the following rotary-cutting techniques. All cutting measurements include a ¼" seam allowance.

1. Begin by folding the fabric in half with the selvage edges together. Place the fabric on your rotary mat so that the entire width of the fabric is on the mat. The folded edge should be closest to you. If you are right-handed, you will be cutting from the left edge of the fabric. If you are left-handed, you will be cutting from the right edge of the fabric. Place the excess fabric on the opposite side from which you will be cutting.

2. Place your long rotary ruler on top of the fabric with one of the lower horizontal lines on the fold. You may find it helpful to use a smaller ruler to the right of your long ruler to act as a

T square. Keep the side of the long ruler as far to the edge of the fabric as possible, allowing you to trim off the smallest amount necessary. Remove the small ruler. Hold the long ruler firmly with your left hand with the rotary cutter in your right hand.

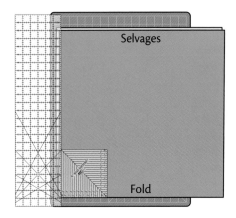

3. Start to cut with the blade *on the mat* and roll it into the fabric. This will ensure that you cut cleanly through the bottom fold of the fabric. Roll the blade away from yourself and keep the fingers of your non-cutting hand on the ruler, not on the fabric. As you cut, keep the blade perpendicular to the side of the ruler so that the side of the blade glides against the ruler. Try not to angle it into the ruler because the blade will rub against the ruler and become dull quickly. It will also distort the edge of your ruler over time, resulting in inaccurate measurements.

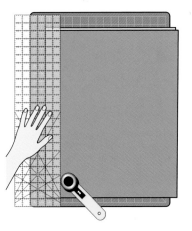

4. After the edge is straightened, cut strips by measuring from the straightened edge. Simply place the required line of your ruler directly on top of the cut edge. Hold the ruler firmly and cut as before. Continue in this manner to cut all required fabric strips.

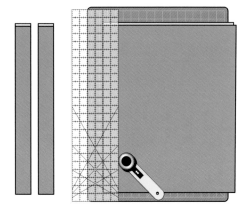

5. After cutting five or six strips, check to see if the edge of your fabric is still perpendicular to the fold. If it has shifted at all, trim as you did in steps 2 and 3 to straighten it again.

Cutting between the Lines

There are some projects in this book that require you to cut increments based on $^{1}/_{16}$". To cut such a measurement, center the raw edge of your fabric between the two appropriate $^{1}/_{8}$" lines on your ruler. For example, if you are instructed to cut a $2^{5}/_{16}$" strip, place the straight raw edge of your fabric between the $2^{1}/_{4}$" and $2^{3}/_{8}$" lines on your ruler.

Cutting Strips into Squares and Rectangles

After you have cut strips into the desired widths, trim the selvage ends from the strip in the same way you trimmed the edge of your yardage. Place the required measurement line on the end of the strip and cut. Continue cutting across the strip until you have the required number of pieces. You can keep the strip folded in half as it was originally so that you will yield two pieces for every cut that you make, or cut each piece individually.

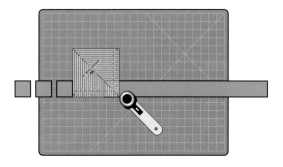

Cutting Half-Square and Quarter-Square Triangles

A half-square triangle is a triangle with the short sides cut on grain. Cutting a square once diagonally yields two half-square triangles. The half-square triangles in this book were calculated by adding $^{7}/_{8}$" to the finished size of the desired triangle. This is the basic formula for figuring the size of the squares and allows for a $^{1}/_{4}$" seam allowance.

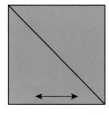
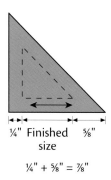

$^{1}/_{4}$"   Finished $^{5}/_{8}$"
size

$^{1}/_{4}$" + $^{5}/_{8}$" = $^{7}/_{8}$"

A quarter-square triangle is a triangle with the long sides cut on grain. Cutting a square twice diagonally yields four quarter-square triangles. The quarter-square triangles in this book were calculated by adding 1¼" to the finished size of the desired triangle. This is the basic formula for figuring the size of the squares and allows for a ¼" seam allowance.

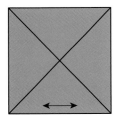

⅝"   Finished   ⅝"
size

Strip Sets

Strip sets are used to simplify the construction process of a quilt. As an example, if you were not using strip sets, a basic 9" finished Nine Patch block would require you to cut nine 3½" squares from two different fabrics and sew them together to make the block.

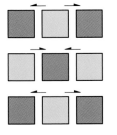

Nine 3½" squares

The strip-set method requires you to make two different strip sets, one for each type of row in the block. For the same block above, strips of the two different colors would be cut 3½" wide and then sewn together along the long edges to make the two strip sets shown above right. The seam allowances are generally pressed toward the darker fabric. After pressing, the strip sets are then cut across the width of the strips, separating them into 3½"-wide segments. Nine Patch blocks generally

use two segments of one strip set and one segment of the other. Finally, you sew the three segments together to complete the block.

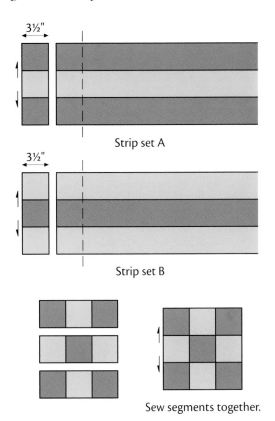

3½"

Strip set A

3½"

Strip set B

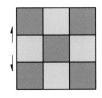

Sew segments together.

The strip-set method eliminates a lot of starting and stopping. It also helps keep the segments and blocks more square because you are handling fewer cut edges in the process of constructing the blocks.

Accurate pressing is the key to making perfect strip sets. Use a hot, *dry* iron to press seam allowances in the direction instructed. You can begin by *lightly* pressing from the wrong side to help establish the direction, but your main pressing needs to be from the right side of the strip set. Use the edge of your iron to get into the folds formed by the seams to make sure that the seams are flat with no pleats. Cutting across a pleat will result in a jagged edge that will not align properly with other pieces of the block.

Cutting Borders on the Lengthwise Grain

Most of the outer borders in this book are cut on the lengthwise grain to ensure stability. To cut such long pieces, I keep the fabric folded in half as for any basic rotary cutting. Then, I fold the yardage in halves, thirds, or quarters so that the *length* of the fabric will fit across my rotary mat. Because I am right-handed, the selvages are to the left side of the fabric.

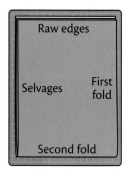

Length of fabric
folded in half

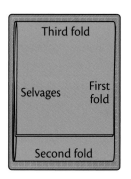

Length of fabric
folded in thirds

To ensure that there is no shifting between the fabric layers, I use the corner of my long plastic ruler and slide it firmly between the folds, pushing the layers tightly together. This extra step can make the difference between long strips that are straight and even or strips that have zigzags in them.

In some cases, as in "Nine by Nine by Nine" (page 65), the outer borders are so long that even if you fold the fabric into quarters, it will still not fit completely across an 18" x 24" mat. Simply cut most of the length needed and then carefully slide the remaining fabric down onto the mat to continue cutting the last few inches. Another option is to use a larger rotary mat. I really like my 24" x 36" mat, especially for cutting extra-long borders. The mat isn't as handy to take to classes but it sure is wonderful to have when I need it!

Accurate Machine Piecing

The single most important aspect of machine piecing is learning to sew and maintain an accurate ¼" seam. There are a few methods that you can use to help with this skill. Most sewing machines now are sold with a ¼" presser foot. It measures ¼" from the needle center to the right edge of the foot. You align the fabric with the edge of the foot when sewing. If your machine does not have one of these presser feet, you can ask your dealer if they sell the foot as a separate attachment. Otherwise, most quilt shops carry generic presser feet that are designed to match the shank style of your sewing machine.

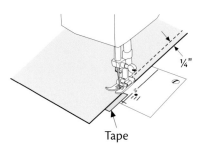

Tape

If you can't find or prefer not to use a ¼" presser foot, you can also mark your machine with a visual guide. Place a piece of masking or white freezer tape ¼" from the needle center. To do this, slide a small piece of graph paper under the unthreaded needle and lower it so that the point goes through the paper directly on the first ¼" line from the edge of the paper. Holding the paper in place, attach the piece of tape to your throat plate, butting it up against the edge of the paper. It can be helpful to extend the tape a few inches in front of the needle so that you can begin to align your fabric as you move it toward the needle.

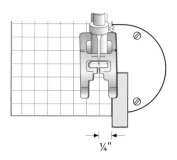

Pressing

I use a steam iron when pressing bulk yardage to help remove any wrinkles or creases before I cut my fabric. However, once I've cut pieces and have started to sew, I only use a hot, *dry* iron.

Moisture significantly relaxes natural fibers like cotton and makes them quite malleable. Often, we use that feature to our advantage if we are sewing clothing, but when pressing quilt blocks or small units, if you use steam, it is very easy to soften the fabric and then set it into a new shape because of the movement of the iron. It is easier to keep blocks and units straight and square using only a hot, dry iron without any steam or moisture.

If you find that you want or need something to help hold a particularly stubborn seam allowance, I recommend using spray sizing, not starch. *Lightly* spray the sizing on the problem area and immediately press, being careful to hold the iron in place for a few seconds. Do not move the iron around.

One final word about pressing: I always press from the *right* side of the units, blocks, or quilt. Even if I begin on the wrong side to help give a sense of direction to the seams, I always finish from the right side. That's the only way that I can check for accuracy and any pleating in the seams.

Assembling the Quilt Top

The quilt top consists of your blocks, sashing (if used), and borders. The quilts in this book use either a straight setting or a diagonal setting.

Straight Settings

Most of the projects in this book use a straight setting. The blocks of straight-set quilts are positioned squarely in horizontal or vertical rows.

1. Lay out the blocks and sashing, if used, referring to the assembly diagram included with each project. Sew the blocks into rows and press the seam allowances as instructed.

2. Sew the rows together. Most times you will be able to butt together or match the block seams. Press the seam allowances as instructed.

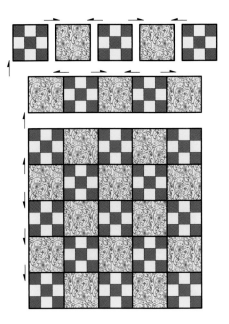

Diagonal Settings

A few quilts in this book, such as "Posy Patch" (page 28) and "Peaceful Retreat" (page 36), use a diagonal or on-point setting. With this setting, the blocks are placed on the diagonal and the spaces around the sides of the quilt top are filled in with side setting triangles and corner setting triangles. Side setting triangles are cut as quarter-square triangles to maintain a straight grain along the outer edges. Corner setting triangles are cut as half-square triangles to achieve a straight grain along the two shorter edges.

1. Lay out the blocks and triangles in diagonal rows as shown in the assembly diagram. Sew the blocks and triangles together in each row. Press the seam allowances as instructed.

2. Sew the rows together and press as instructed. Finally, add the remaining corner triangles and press as instructed to complete the quilt top.

Adding Borders

Most of the quilts in this book have simple borders. That means border strips are sewn to opposite sides and then two more border strips are sewn to the top and bottom of the quilt. Sometimes you will see these borders referred to as butted borders.

I have given sizes for all borders in the book. It is usually best to sew borders to a quilt with the border strip on the bottom next to the feed dogs and the quilt top, wrong side up, on top. Sewing in this manner means that you can see the seams and seam intersections to ensure that everything stays in the proper position. If the quilt top is on the bottom, it is likely that some of the seam allowances will catch on the feed dogs and get turned in the wrong direction.

When I sew a border strip to a quilt, I first fold the raw edge of the border into quarters, lightly crease the folds, and mark the creases with a pin. Then, I do the same for the side of the quilt. When I pin the border to the quilt, I match pin points, as

well as matching the ends of the quilt and border. Then I fill in along the edge with enough pins to hold the layers together when I sew.

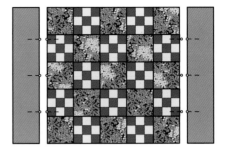

Pin-mark.

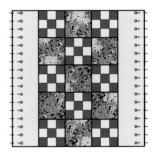

Sew the side borders to the quilt top first. Press the seam allowances toward the border strips. Repeat for the top and bottom borders.

Multiple rounds of borders are sewn to the quilt in the same way. You can see in "Nine Patch Medallion" (page 40) that there are three rounds of plain borders between each round of pieced borders.

Some quilts, such as "Sky Gems" (page 32) and "Some Like It Hot" (page 48), have pieced blocks in the corners of the borders. These borders are basically the same style as the simple borders described above but require some additional steps, which are include in the project instructions.

"Nearly Neutral" (page 24) has pieced borders as well as border blocks. You will see that these borders are constructed using strip-set segments. This is a fun look and is quite an easy way to add additional interest to any quilt.

"Nine by Nine by Nine" (page 65) is the only quilt in the book that has mitered borders. This is because I wanted to have the striped pattern continue around the edge of the quilt without interruption. I have given specific instructions within that project that will help you with the mitering process.

Finishing the Quilt

Now that the quilt top is completed you are ready to move on to the final steps. Often you will hear the layers of a quilt referred to as the quilt "sandwich." This sandwich consists of three layers—quilt top, batting, and backing.

Preparing the Backing

The prepared backing should measure 4" to 6" larger than the quilt top. This will allow for any shifting that may occur in the basting and quilting process.

You will notice in the materials list for each project that next to the backing fabric yardage I have noted the number of widths to cut from the yardage and the way the pieces should be seamed together, with either vertical or horizontal seams, based on the most efficient use of the yardage.

When possible, I like to have a full panel of fabric centered on the back of a quilt with any seams placed equidistant from the center panel. When working with two widths of fabric, the easiest way that I have found to do this is to sew the two panels together along both outside edges that are parallel to the selvages, right sides together. Use a generous seam allowance so that you are not catching the selvage in the seam. Then, trim the seam allowances to ½" or so. (You can "eyeball" this and cut them with scissors if you don't want to get out your rotary equipment.) Snip the top at the center of *one* of the panels and then tear down the

length of the panel at the snip. Press the seam allowances open. You're finished!

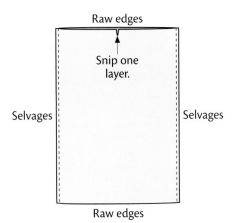

Preparing backing using two widths of fabric

When sewing three widths of fabric together, you will automatically have three equal-sized widths that will enable you to place the seams equidistant from the center panel of the back of the quilt.

Batting

Batting should also be 4" to 6" larger than the quilt top. I prefer to use cotton or cotton-blend battings. I like putting a natural-fiber batting inside my cotton quilts. Then all the fibers can "breathe" together! You will find many brands available at your local quilt shop. I look for brands that allow you to space your quilting lines up to 8" or 10" apart. This is especially helpful if you don't have the time or interest to do heavy quilting.

If you buy packaged batting, unfold it and lay it out to relax for at least a day. Sometimes I put the batting into my dryer on low heat with a damp cloth to help steam out some of the wrinkles.

Putting the Layers Together

Find a large, flat area to layer your quilt. I have several places that work well for me, depending on the size of the quilt. I use the island in my kitchen quite a bit, as well as my Ping-Pong table. If all else fails, there's always the kitchen floor, but my knees don't appreciate that very much!

1. Center the prepared backing on the work surface, wrong side up. Use pieces of masking tape to anchor the corners and edges of the backing so that it doesn't slide around while you are working.

2. Layer and smooth the batting over the backing. Be careful that there are no wrinkles.

3. Place the pressed quilt top over the batting, right side up. Take your time to smooth the quilt top, checking that the quilt blocks and seams are straight in all directions.

4. If you are hand quilting, baste the layers together with needle and thread. I like to use a *fine* darning needle that is about 4" long. It helps me take big stitches, which are easier to take out when the quilting is completed. I use cotton thread that contrasts with the fabrics in my quilt top, again making it easier when it's time to remove the basting stitches. Baste the layers together in a grid, using horizontal and vertical stitching placed 6" to 8" apart. Stitch around the outside edges of the quilt top as the final step.

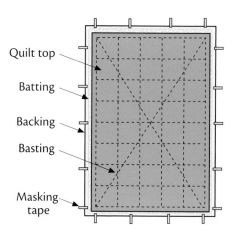

If you are machine quilting, use stainless steel or brass safety pins to pin the quilt layers together. I prefer a size 2 safety pin because I find it easy to open and close. You can use several hundred safety pins on a large quilt, so easy opening is an important detail! Try to place the pins approximately 6" apart, avoiding any areas that may potentially contain quilting lines.

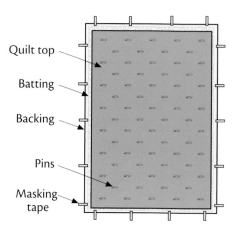

Quilting by Hand or Machine

For specific instruction on hand quilting, refer to *Quilting Makes the Quilt* by Lee Cleland (Martingale & Company, 1994). For specific instruction on machine quilting, refer to *Machine Quilting Made Easy!* by Maurine Noble (Martingale & Company, 1994).

Binding the Quilt

Most of these quilts use straight-grain binding. In fact, the only quilt that uses bias binding is "Perkiomen Valley Nine Patch" (page 56). Brief instructions for bias binding are included with that project.

Whether using straight-grain or bias binding, I prefer to use a double-fold binding, sometimes referred to as French binding. This gives added durability to the edge of a quilt, which is often the part of a quilt that gets the most wear.

The instructions for each project include the amount of yardage and the number of strips that you will need to cut to make your binding. I have allowed enough fabric to go around the perimeter of the quilt plus 10" to 12" extra.

1. With right sides together, sew the binding strips together at right angles as shown to make one continuous strip. Trim the excess ¼" from each stitching line and press the seam allowances open.

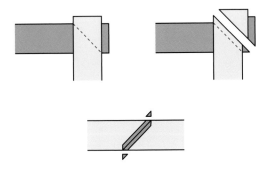

2. Press the pieced strip in half, *wrong sides together,* being careful not to stretch the binding.

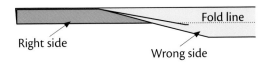

Right side
Fold line
Wrong side

3. Place the binding at the bottom edge of the quilt between the middle and a corner, aligning the raw edges. Beginning about 4" from the binding end, stitch the binding in place, using a ¼" seam. Stop stitching a generous ¼" from the corner and backstitch. Remove the quilt from the sewing machine. Fold the binding up and away from the quilt, keeping all raw edges aligned. Fold the strip back down, aligning the fold with the edge of the quilt.

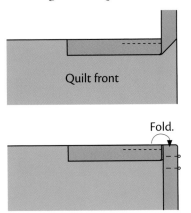

Quilt front

Fold.

4. Start sewing at the fold and continue to the next corner. Miter all corners in the same manner.

5. Stop sewing about 10" from the beginning point. Take the quilt out of the sewing machine. Fold back and crease or press the end of the binding strip so that the fold is butted against the cut edge of the beginning of the strip. Unfold the strip and cut 2½" (the width of the binding) away from the fold toward the end of the strip.

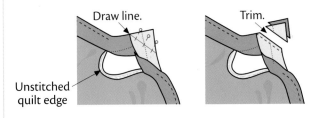

2½"
Beginning edge of binding

Fold back end of binding even with the beginning edge.
Cut 2½" from the fold.

6. Unfold both ends of the binding and place the ends perpendicular to each other, right sides together. Pin the ends together as shown. Draw a diagonal line from one corner to the opposite corner. Sew on the line. Trim ¼" from the stitching line and press the seam allowance open.

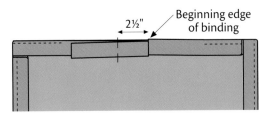

Draw line.
Trim.
Unstitched quilt edge

7. Refold the binding. Align the raw edges of the binding with the edge of the quilt top and finish sewing the binding in place.

8. Fold the binding to the back of the quilt. Using a matching thread color, hand blindstitch the binding to the quilt, mitering the corners.

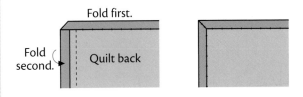

Fold first.
Fold second.
Quilt back

nearly NEUTRAL

FINISHED QUILT:
66½" X 84½"

FINISHED LARGE NINE
PATCH BLOCKS: 9" X 9"

FINISHED SMALL NINE
PATCH BLOCKS: 6" X 6"

Designed and pieced by Cyndi Hershey. Quilted by Angela Baker.

Sometimes simple construction and comfortable colors are all that's needed to create a wonderful quilt design. The two neutral color families used for the Nine Patch blocks help produce the calm and peaceful effect of this quilt. However, you could use a light and dark value of any two color families to make your own unique version.

Materials

Yardage is based on 42"-wide fabric.

- 1⅝ yards *each* of dark gray and dark brown batiks for blocks and outer border
- 1½ yards of light brown batik for blocks, sashing squares, and outer border
- 1⅜ yards of light gray batik for blocks and outer border
- 1⅓ yards of rust multicolored batik for sashing and binding
- ⅝ yard of rust tonal batik for inner border
- 5¼ yards of fabric for backing (2 widths pieced lengthwise)
- 72" x 90" piece of batting

Cutting

All measurements include ¼"-wide seam allowances.

From *each* of the dark gray and dark brown batiks, cut:

- 14 strips, 3½" x 42" (28 total)
- 1 strip, 2½" x 42"; crosscut into 3 strips, 2½" x 14" (6 total)

From the light gray batik, cut:

- 12 strips, 3½" x 42"
- 1 strip, 2½" x 42"; crosscut into 3 strips, 2½" x 14"

From the light brown batik, cut:

- 12 strips, 3½" x 42"
- 1 strip, 2½" x 42"; crosscut into 3 strips, 2½" x 14"
- 1 strip, 1½" x 42"; crosscut into 24 squares, 1½" x 1½"

From the rust multicolored batik, cut:

- 15 strips, 1½" x 42"; crosscut into 58 rectangles, 1½" x 9½"
- 8 strips, 2½" x 42"

From the rust tonal batik, cut:

- 4 strips, 3" x 42"
- 3 strips, 2" x 42"

Making the Large Nine Patch Blocks

1. Sew dark gray and light gray 3½" x 42" strips together as shown to make strip sets A and B. Make the amount indicated for each strip set. Press the seam allowances toward the dark gray strips. Crosscut strip sets A into 36 segments and strip sets B into 18 segments, each 3½" wide.

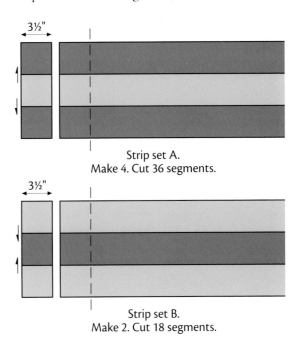

3½"

Strip set A.
Make 4. Cut 36 segments.

3½"

Strip set B.
Make 2. Cut 18 segments.

2. Sew two A segments and one B segment together as shown to make one block. Press the seam allowances toward the A segments. Repeat to make a total of 18 blocks.

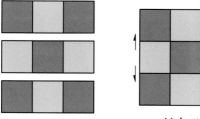

Make 18.

3. Repeat steps 1 and 2 using dark brown and light brown 3½" x 42" strips. Make the same amount of strip sets, but cut strip sets A into 34 segments and strip sets B into 17 segments. Make a total of 17 blocks.

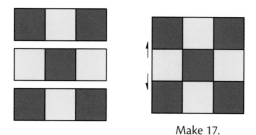

Make 17.

Assembling the Quilt Top

1. Lay out the blocks and the rust multicolored 1½" x 9½" rectangles as shown to make block rows 1 and 2. Make four of row 1 and three of row 2. Press the seam allowances toward the rectangles.

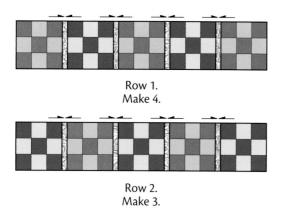

Row 1.
Make 4.

Row 2.
Make 3.

2. To make the sashing rows, sew five rust multi-colored 1½" x 9½" rectangles and four light brown batik 1½" squares together as shown. Make six rows. Press the seam allowances toward the rectangles.

Sashing row.
Make 6.

3. Refer to the assembly diagram (page 27) to sew the block rows and sashing rows together to complete the quilt center. Press the seam allowances toward the sashing rows.

Making and Adding the Borders

1. Sew the rust tonal batik 3" x 42" strips together end to end and press the seam allowances open. From the pieced strip, cut two 3" x 69½" strips. Sew these strips to the sides of the quilt center. Press the seam allowances toward the border strips. Sew the rust tonal batik 2" x 42" strips together end to end and press the seam allowances open. From the pieced strip, cut two 2" x 54½" strips. Sew these strips to the top and bottom of the quilt center. Press the seam allowances toward the border strips.

2. Sew the remaining 3½" x 42" strips together in the order shown to make a strip set. Make four. Press the seam allowances in one direction. Crosscut the strip sets into 21 segments, 6½" wide.

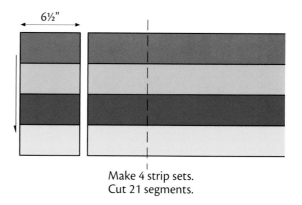

6½"

Make 4 strip sets.
Cut 21 segments.

3. Remove the center seam from two of the step 2 segments to create four half-segments.

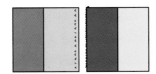

Remove stitching to
make 4 half-segments.

4. Sew the full border segments and the half border segments together as shown to make the outer-border strips, being careful to follow the correct color order. Press the seam allowances in the same direction as the previous seams.

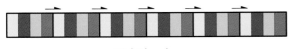

Right border

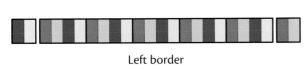

Left border

Top border

Bottom border

5. Refer to the assembly diagram to sew the side borders to the quilt, being careful to position them correctly. Press the seam allowances toward the inner borders.

6. Using the 2½"-wide dark gray and light gray strips, refer to steps 1 and 2 of "Making the Large Nine Patch Blocks" (page 25) to make one each of strip sets A and B. Crosscut strip set A into four segments and strip set B into two segments, each 2½" wide. Sew the segments together to make two border–corner blocks.

7. Repeat step 6 with the 2½"-wide dark brown and light brown strips to make two border-corner blocks.

8. Referring to the assembly diagram for proper placement, sew the border-corner blocks to the ends of the top and bottom borders. Press the seam allowances toward the blocks. Sew the borders to the top and bottom of the quilt. Press the seam allowances toward the inner borders.

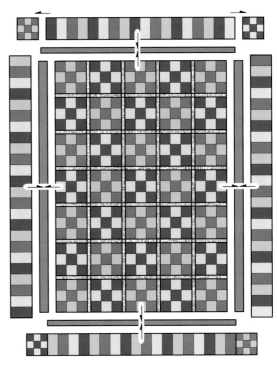

Quilt assembly

Finishing the Quilt

1. Layer your quilt with batting and pieced backing; baste. Quilt as desired. The project quilt was quilted with various feather motifs throughout the quilt. The curves of the quilting provide a nice balance to the many angles of the piecing.

2. Trim the edges of the quilt layers even with the quilt top. Use the rust multicolored 2½" x 42" strips to bind the quilt.

POSY PATCH

FINISHED QUILT:
78¼" X 91"

FINISHED BLOCKS:
9" X 9"

Designed by Cyndi Hershey. Pieced by Doris Adomsky. Quilted by Pat Burns.

Have you ever seen a fabric collection displayed so beautifully in a quilt shop that you wanted all the fabrics? This quilt uses many pieces from one folk-art themed fabric collection. The simplicity of the overall design and the large pieces allow the individual fabrics to really shine.

Materials

Yardage is based on 42"-wide fabric.

- 2½ yards of purple large-scale floral print for outer border
- 2⅛ yards of purple small-scale floral print for alternate blocks and binding
- 1⅝ yards of yellow-and-red star print for blocks
- 1⅓ yards of red star print for blocks
- 1⅓ yards of purple star print for setting triangles
- ½ yard of yellow-and-red striped print for inner border
- 7½ yards of fabric for backing (3 widths pieced crosswise)
- 84" x 97" piece of batting

Cutting

All measurements include ¼"-wide seam allowances.

From the yellow-and-red star print, cut:

- 15 strips, 3½" x 42"

From the red star print, cut:

- 12 strips, 3½" x 42"

From the purple small-scale floral print, cut:

- 5 strips, 9½" x 42"; crosscut into 20 squares, 9½" x 9½"
- 9 strips, 2½" x 42"

From the purple star print, cut:

- 3 strips, 14" x 42"; crosscut into 5 squares, 14" x 14". Cut each square twice diagonally to yield 20 quarter-square triangles. You will use 18. From the remainder of 1 strip, cut 2 squares, 7¼" x 7¼". Cut each square once diagonally to yield 4 half-square triangles.

From the yellow-and-red striped print, cut:

- 8 strips, 1½" x 42"

From the purple large-scale floral print, cut:

- 2 strips, 6½" x 78¼", along the *lengthwise* grain
- 2 strips, 6½" x 79", along the *lengthwise* grain

Making the Blocks

1. Sew the yellow-and-red and red star print 3½" x 42" strips together as shown to make strip sets A and B. Make the amount indicated for each strip set. Press the seam allowances toward the red strips. Crosscut strip sets A into 60 segments and strip sets B into 30 segments, each 3½" wide.

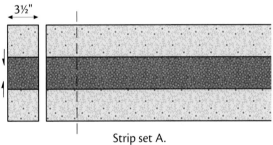

Strip set A.
Make 6. Cut 60 segments.

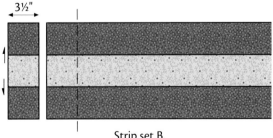

Strip set B.
Make 3. Cut 30 segments.

2. Sew two A segments and one B segment together as shown to make one block. Press the seam allowances toward the A segments. Repeat to make a total of 30 Nine Patch blocks.

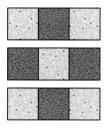 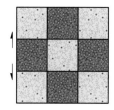

Make 30.

Assembling the Quilt Top

Refer to the assembly diagram at right to lay out the Nine Patch blocks, purple floral 9½" alternate blocks, and purple star print setting triangles in diagonal rows. Join the pieces in each row. Press the seam allowances toward the alternate blocks and setting triangles. Sew the rows together. Press the seam allowances away from the center diagonal row. Add the remaining corner triangles to complete the quilt.

Adding the Borders

1. Sew the striped 1½" x 42" strips together end to end and press the seam allowances open. From the pieced strip, cut two 1½" x 77" strips for the side inner borders and two 1½" x 66¼" strips for the top and bottom inner borders. Sew the side borders to the quilt center. Press the seam allowances toward the border strips. Sew the top and bottom borders to the quilt center. Press the seam allowances toward the border strips.

2. Sew a purple large-scale floral 6½" x 79" strip to the sides of the quilt. Press the seam allowances toward the outer-border strips. Sew a purple large-scale floral 6½" x 78¼" strip to the top and bottom of the quilt. Press the seam allowances toward the outer-border strips.

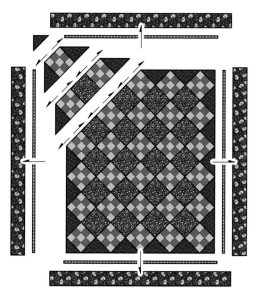

Quilt assembly

Finishing the Quilt

1. Layer your quilt with batting and pieced backing; baste. Quilt as desired. The large blocks and setting triangles offer a great canvas to showcase your creative quilting ideas!

2. Trim the edges of the quilt layers even with the quilt top. Use the purple small-scale floral 2½" x 42" strips to bind the quilt.

Alternative fabric selections

Sky GEMS

FINISHED QUILT:
41" X 41"

FINISHED SQUARE-IN-A-SQUARE BLOCK:
9" X 9"

FINISHED NINE PATCH SASHING BLOCK:
2¼" X 2¼"

FINISHED NINE PATCH BORDER BLOCK:
4½" X 4½"

Designed and quilted by Cyndi Hershey. Pieced by Doris Adomsky.

Light up any room with this vibrantly colored quilt. Companion large- and small-scale firework prints with metallic accents provide bursts of interest in the block centers and border, while bright but subtle prints provide the backdrop. The Square-in-a-Square block design lends itself to any busy or large-scale theme print, and the Nine Patch blocks in the sashing and border provide definition without competing for attention with the busy theme fabrics.

Materials

Yardage is based on 42"-wide fabric.

- 1 yard of large-scale firework print for border and backing
- ⅞ yard of small-scale firework print for block centers and binding
- ½ yard of red striped print for blocks, sashing blocks, and border blocks
- ½ yard of blue striped print for blocks, sashing blocks, and border blocks
- ⅓ yard of black solid for sashing and sashing blocks
- ⅓ yard of yellow swirl print for sashing and border blocks
- 1⅛ yards of fabric for backing (full piece bordered by outer-border fabric to achieve needed size)
- 47" x 47" square of batting

Cutting

All measurements include ¼"-wide seam allowances.

From the small-scale firework print, cut:

- 2 strips, 6⅞" x 42"; crosscut into 9 squares, 6⅞" x 6⅞"
- 5 strips, 2½" x 42"

From the red striped print, cut:

- 2 strips, 5⅜" x 42"; crosscut into 10 squares, 5⅜" x 5⅜". Cut 5 squares once diagonally from the lower-left corner to the upper-right corner to yield 10 A half-square triangles. Cut the remaining 5 squares once diagonally from the lower-right corner to the upper-left corner to yield 10 B half-square triangles.
- 1 strip, 1¼" x 42"; crosscut into 16 squares, 1¼" x 1¼"
- 1 strip, 2" x 42"; crosscut in half. You will use 1 half.

From the blue striped print, cut:

- 2 strips, 5⅜" x 42"; crosscut into 8 squares, 5⅜" x 5⅜". Cut 4 squares once diagonally from the lower-left corner to the upper-right corner to yield 8 A half-square triangles. Cut the remaining 4 squares once diagonally from the lower-right corner to the upper-left corner to yield 8 B half-square triangles.
- 1 strip, 1¼" x 42"; crosscut into 4 squares, 1¼" x 1¼"
- 1 strip, 2" x 42"; crosscut in half

From the black solid, cut:

- 7 strips, 1¼" x 42"; crosscut *1* strip into 16 squares, 1¼" x 1¼"

From the yellow swirl print, cut:

- 3 strips, 1¼" x 42"
- 2 strips, 2" x 42"; crosscut each strip in half. You will use 3 halves.

From the large-scale firework print, cut:

- 4 strips, 5" x 32", along the *lengthwise* grain

Making the Blocks

1. Sew red striped A triangles to opposite sides of a small-scale firework print 6⅞" square. Press the seam allowances toward the triangles. Sew red striped B triangles to the remaining sides of the square. Press the seam allowances toward the triangles. The stripes should be arranged so they are running in the same direction. Repeat to make a total of five red Square-in-a-Square blocks.

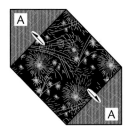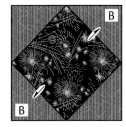

Make 5.

2. Repeat step 1 using the blue striped triangles and the remaining 6⅞" squares. Make a total of four blue Square-in-a-Square blocks.

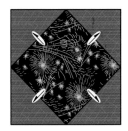

Make 4.

Assembling the Quilt Top

1. Sew the black and yellow swirl 1¼" x 42" strips together as shown to make strip set A. Make three. Press the seam allowances toward the black strips. Crosscut the strip sets into 12 sashing segments, 9½" wide.

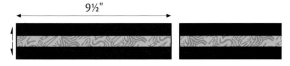

Strip set A.
Make 3. Cut 12 segments.

2. Lay out four red striped 1¼" squares, one blue striped 1¼" square, and four black 1¼" squares in three horizontal rows. Pay careful attention to the direction of the striped squares. Sew the squares in each row together. Press the seam allowances toward the black squares. Join the rows and press the seam allowances toward the outer rows. Repeat to make a total of four sashing blocks.

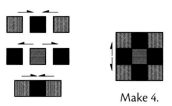

Make 4.

3. To make the block rows, lay out the Square-in-a-Square blocks and sashing segments in three rows, paying attention to the direction of the striped fabrics. The red stripes should run vertical and the blue stripes should run horizontal. Press the seam allowances toward the sashing segments.

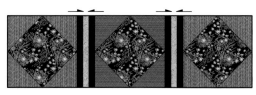

Make 2.

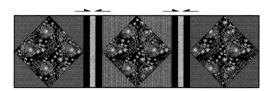

Make 1.

4. To make the sashing rows, join two sashing blocks and three sashing segments. Press the seam allowances toward the sashing segments. Repeat to make a total of two rows.

Make 2.

5. Refer to the assembly diagram below right to sew a sashing row between each of the block rows. Press the seam allowances toward the sashing rows.

Making and Adding the Border

1. Sew the blue, yellow, and red 2"-wide half strips together as shown to make one *each* of strip sets B and C. Press the seam allowances toward the blue and red strips. Crosscut strip set B into eight segments and strip set C into four segments, each 2" wide.

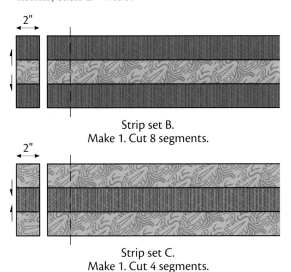

Strip set B.
Make 1. Cut 8 segments.

Strip set C.
Make 1. Cut 4 segments.

2. Sew two B segments and one C segment together as shown to make one block. Press the seam allowances toward the B segments. Repeat to make a total of four border blocks.

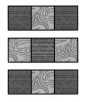

Make 4.

3. Sew a large-scale firework print 5" x 32" strip to the sides of the quilt center. Press the seam allowances toward the border strips.

4. Sew a border block to each end of the remaining large-scale firework print strips. Press the seam allowances toward the border strips. Sew these borders to the top and bottom of the quilt center. Press the seam allowances toward the borders.

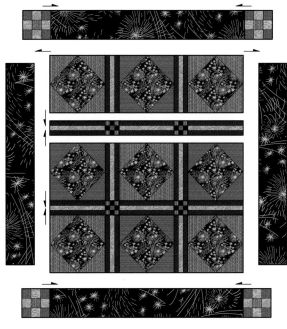

Quilt assembly

Finishing the Quilt

1. Use the remaining large-scale firework print to border the backing fabric to make a backing piece that is 47" square.

2. Layer your quilt with batting and pieced backing; baste. Quilt as desired.

3. Trim the edges of the quilt layers even with the quilt top. Use the small-scale firework print 2½" x 42" strips to bind the quilt.

Peaceful RETREAT

FINISHED QUILT:
65½" X 78¼"

FINISHED OHIO STAR BLOCK:
9" X 9"

FINISHED NINE PATCH BLOCK:
4½" X 4½"

Designed by Cyndi Hershey. Pieced by Doris Adomsky. Quilted by Pat Burns.

Balance is created in this bar quilt by using Nine Patch blocks that are half the size of the Ohio Star blocks. Additionally, the Ohio Star blocks are from the nine-patch category of pieced blocks. The fabric choices were based on an analogous color scheme, which uses colors that lie next to each other on the color wheel. This color "recipe" is one of the easiest ones to use and really helps give a sense of style to any quilt.

Materials

Yardage is based on 42"-wide fabric.

- 2⅓ yards of blueberry print for Ohio Star rows and binding
- 2 yards of dark multicolored print for outer border
- 1¼ yards of light blue fabric for Ohio Star blocks
- ⅞ yard of medium blue fabric for Ohio Star blocks
- ⅝ yard of medium green dot print for Nine Patch block rows
- ⅜ yard of dark green fabric for Nine Patch blocks
- ⅓ yard of light green fabric for Nine Patch blocks
- ⅓ yard of yellow fabric for inner border
- 5 yards of fabric for backing (2 widths pieced lengthwise)
- 71" x 84" piece of batting

Cutting

All measurements include ¼"-wide seam allowances.

From the medium blue fabric, cut:

- 4 strips, 4¼" x 42"; crosscut into 30 squares, 4¼" x 4¼". Cut each square twice diagonally to yield 120 quarter-square triangles.
- 2 strips, 3½" x 42"; crosscut into 15 squares, 3½" x 3½"

From the light blue fabric, cut:

- 4 strips, 4¼" x 42"; crosscut into 30 squares, 4¼" x 4¼". Cut each square twice diagonally to yield 120 quarter-square triangles.
- 6 strips, 3½" x 42"; crosscut into 60 squares, 3½" x 3½"

From the blueberry print, cut:

- 3 strips, 14" x 42"; crosscut into 6 squares, 14" x 14". Cut each square twice diagonally to yield 24 quarter-square triangles.
- 2 strips, 7¼" x 42"; crosscut into 6 squares, 7¼" x 7¼". Cut each square once diagonally to yield 12 half-square triangles.
- 8 strips, 2½" x 42"

From the dark green fabric, cut:

- 5 strips, 2" x 42"

From the light green fabric, cut:

- 4 strips, 2" x 42"

From the medium green dot print, cut:

- 2 strips, 7⅝" x 42"; crosscut into 9 squares, 7⅝" x 7⅝". Cut each square twice diagonally to yield 36 quarter-square triangles.
- 1 strip, 4¹/₁₆" x 42"; crosscut into 4 squares, 4¹/₁₆" x 4¹/₁₆". Cut each square once diagonally to yield 8 half-square triangles.

From the yellow fabric, cut:

- 6 strips, 1½" x 42"

From the dark multicolored print, cut:

- 2 strips, 6½" x 66¼", along the *lengthwise* grain
- 2 strips, 6½" x 65½", along the *lengthwise* grain

Making the Ohio Star Block Rows

1. Sew each medium blue 4¼" triangle to a light blue 4¼" triangle as shown. Press the seam allowances toward the medium blue triangles. Sew two units together to make a pieced square. Press the seam allowance in either direction. Repeat to make a total of 60 quarter-square-triangle units.

Make 120.   Make 60.

2. Lay out four quarter-square-triangle units, four light blue 3½" squares, and one medium blue 3½" square in three rows. Sew the units in each row together. Press the seam allowances toward the squares. Sew the rows together. Press the seam allowances toward the outer rows. Repeat to make a total of 15 Ohio Star blocks.

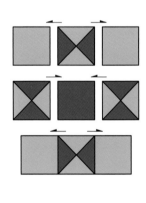

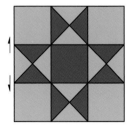

Make 15.

3. Lay out five Ohio Star blocks, eight blueberry print quarter-square triangles, and four blueberry print half-square triangles in diagonal rows. Sew the blocks and triangles in each row together. Press the seam allowances toward the triangles. Join the rows. Press the seam allowances in one direction. Add the remaining half-square triangles to the corners to complete one block row. Press the seam allowances toward the corner triangles. Repeat to make a total of three rows.

Make 3.

Making the Nine Patch Block Rows

1. Sew the dark green and light green 2" x 42" strips together as shown to make strip sets A and B. Make the amount indicated for each strip set. Press the seam allowances toward the dark green strips. Crosscut strip sets A into 40 segments and strip set B into 20 segments, each 2" wide.

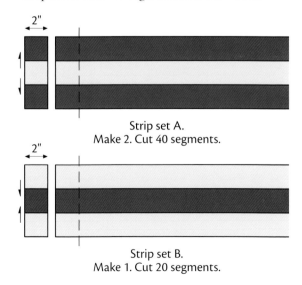

Strip set A.
Make 2. Cut 40 segments.

Strip set B.
Make 1. Cut 20 segments.

2. Sew two A segments and one B segment together as shown to make one block. Press the seam allowances toward the A segments. Repeat to make a total of 20 Nine Patch blocks.

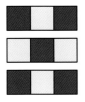

Make 20.

3. Lay out 10 Nine Patch blocks, 18 medium green dot quarter-square triangles, and four medium green dot half-square triangles in diagonal rows. Sew the blocks and triangles in each row together. Press the seam allowances toward the triangles. Join the rows. Press the seam allowances in one direction. Add the remaining half-square triangles to the corners to complete one Nine Patch block row. Press the seam allowances toward the corner triangles. Repeat to make a total of two rows.

Make 2.

Assembling the Quilt Top

1. Refer to the quilt assembly diagram above right the seam allowances toward the Nine Patch block rows.

2. Sew the yellow 1½" x 42" strips together end to end and press the seam allowances open. From the pieced strip, cut two 1½" x 64¼" strips for the inner side borders and two

1½" x 53½" strips for the inner top and bottom borders. Sew the side borders to the quilt center. Press the seam allowances toward the border strips. Sew the top and bottom borders to the quilt center. Press the seam allowances toward the border strips.

3. Sew the dark multicolored 6½" x 66¼" strips to the sides of the quilt. Press the seam allowances toward the outer borders. Sew the dark multicolored 6½" x 65½" strips to the top and bottom of the quilt. Press the seam allowances toward the outer borders.

Quilt assembly

Finishing the Quilt

1. Layer your quilt with batting and pieced backing; baste. Quilt as desired. Both sizes of setting triangles offer terrific places to showcase some special quilting designs.

2. Trim the edges of the quilt layers even with the quilt top. Use the blueberry print 2½" x 42" strips to bind the quilt.

Nine Patch
MEDALLION

FINISHED
QUILT:
115½" X 115½"

Designed and pieced by Cyndi Hershey. Quilted by Kim Pope.

A medallion quilt is made of rounds of borders that frame a center focal block or unit. In this case, the border rounds contain Nine Patch blocks set straight and on point, as well as a checkerboard that is a variation of multiple Nine Patch blocks. The Florentine style of the prints emphasizes the tiled look of this quilt design.

Materials

Yardage is based on 42"-wide fabric.

- 4¼ yards of purple floral print for center unit, border blocks, and outer border
- 3⅜ yards of cream multicolored print for center unit and setting triangles
- 2⅝ yards of dark purple print for checkerboard border, frames, and border blocks
- 2⅝ yards of yellow print for frames
- 2 yards of dark red print for border blocks
- 1⅝ yards of medium purple print for checkerboard border and binding
- ⅔ yard of orange print for frames
- ⅝ yard of light red print for border blocks
- 10½ yards of fabric for backing (3 widths pieced in either direction)
- 121" x 121" square of batting

Cutting

All measurements include ¼"-wide seam allowances.

From the purple floral print, cut:

- 1 square, 14⅝" x 14⅝"
- 2 strips, 3½" x 42"; crosscut into 20 squares, 3½" x 3½"

From the *remainder* of the purple floral print, cut:

- 2 strips, 8½" x 99½", along the *lengthwise* grain
- 2 strips, 8½" x 115½", along the *lengthwise* grain

From the cream multicolored print, cut:

- 1 strip, 10⅞" x 42"; crosscut into 2 squares, 10⅞" x 10⅞". Cut each square once diagonally to yield 4 half-square triangles.
- 8 strips, 10¼" x 42"; crosscut into 22 squares, 10¼" x 10¼". Cut each square twice diagonally to yield 88 quarter-square triangles.
- 3 strips, 5⅜" x 42"; crosscut into 16 squares, 5⅜" x 5⅜". Cut each square once diagonally to yield 32 half-square triangles.

From the orange print, cut:

- 3 strips, 2½" x 42"
- 7 strips, 2" x 42"

From the dark purple print, cut:

- 7 strips, 2½" x 42"
- 13 strips, 2⅝" x 42"
- 2 strips, 2" x 39½"
- 12 strips, 2" x 42"
- 2 strips, 3½" x 42"; crosscut into 16 squares, 3½" x 3½"

From the medium purple print, cut:

- 20 strips, 2½" x 42"

From the yellow print, cut:

- 2 strips, 2" x 36½"
- 2 strips, 2" x 39½"
- 38 strips, 2" x 42"

From the dark red print, cut:

- 19 strips, 2⅝" x 42"
- 4 strips, 3½" x 42"; crosscut into 36 squares, 3½" x 3½"

From the light red print, cut:

- 7 strips, 2⅝" x 42"

Making the Center Block and Frame

1. Sew cream multicolored 10⅞" triangles to opposite sides of the purple floral print 14⅝" square. Press the seam allowances toward the triangles. Repeat on the remaining sides of the triangle.

Make 1.

2. Sew the orange print 2½" x 42" strips together end to end and press the seam allowances open. From the pieced strip, cut two 2½" x 20½" strips and two 2½" x 24½" strips. Sew the 2½" x 20½" strips to the sides of the center block. Press the seam allowances toward the orange strips. Sew the 2½" x 24½" strips to the top and bottom of the center block. Press the seam allowances toward the orange strips.

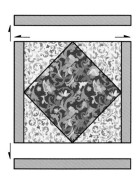

Making the Checkerboard Border and Frames

1. Sew the dark purple 2½" x 42" strips and eight of the medium purple 2½" x 42" strips together as shown to make strip sets A and B. Make the amount indicated for each strip set. Press the seam allowances toward the dark purple strips.

Crosscut strip sets A into 24 segments and strip sets B into 36 segments, each 2½" wide.

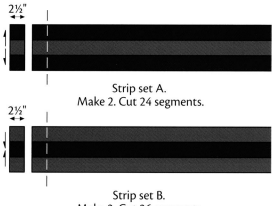

2½"

Strip set A.
Make 2. Cut 24 segments.

2½"

Strip set B.
Make 3. Cut 36 segments.

2. Sew the A and B segments together as shown to make two side borders and two top/bottom borders. Press the seam allowances as shown.

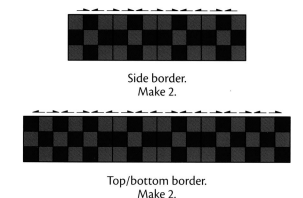

Side border.
Make 2.

Top/bottom border.
Make 2.

3. Sew the checkerboard side borders to the sides of the quilt center. Press the seam allowances toward the orange strips. Sew the checkerboard top and bottom borders to the quilt center. Press the seam allowances toward the orange strips.

4. Sew the yellow 2" x 36½" strips to the sides of the quilt. Press the seam allowances toward the yellow strips. Sew the yellow 2" x 39½" strips to the top and bottom of the quilt. Press the seam allowances toward the yellow strips.

5. Sew the dark purple 2" x 39½" strips to the sides of the quilt. Press the seam allowances toward the dark purple strips. Sew the dark purple 2" x 42" strips together end to end and press the seam allowances open. From the pieced strip, cut two 2" x 42½" strips and sew them to the top and bottom of the quilt. Press the seam allowances toward the dark purple strips. Set the remainder of the pieced strip aside.

6. Sew the yellow 2" x 42" strips together end to end and press the seam allowances open. From the pieced strip, cut two 2" x 42½" strips and two 2" x 45½" strips. Set the remainder of the pieced strip aside. Sew the 2" x 42½" strips to the sides of the quilt. Press the seam allowances toward the dark purple strips. Sew the yellow 2" x 45½" strips to the top and bottom of the quilt. Press the seam allowances toward the dark purple strips.

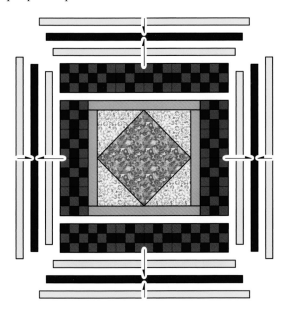

Making the Red Border Blocks and Frames

1. Sew the light red 2⅝" x 42" strips and eight of the dark red 2⅝" x 42" strips together as shown to make strip sets C and D. Make the amount indicated for each strip set. Press the seam

allowances toward the dark red strips. Crosscut strip sets C into 40 segments and strip sets D into 20 segments, each 2⅝" wide.

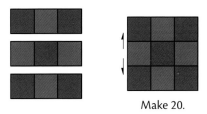

2⅝"

Strip set C.
Make 3. Cut 40 segments.

2⅝"

Strip set D.
Make 2. Cut 20 segments.

2. Sew two C segments and one D segment together as shown to make one block. Press the seam allowances toward the C segments. Repeat to make a total of 20 Nine Patch blocks.

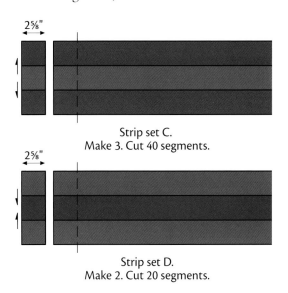

Make 20.

3. Lay out five Nine Patch blocks, eight cream multicolored quarter-square triangles, and four cream multicolored half-square triangles in diagonal rows. Sew the blocks and triangles in each row together. Press the seam allowances toward the triangles. Join the rows. Press the seam allowances in one direction. Add the remaining half-square triangles to the corners. Press the seam allowances toward the corner triangles. Repeat to make a total of four borders.

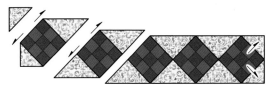

Make 4.

4. To make the border corner blocks, lay out the purple floral print and dark red 3½" squares in three rows as shown. Sew the squares in each row together. Press the seam allowances toward the dark red squares. Sew the rows together. Press the seam allowances toward the middle row. Repeat to make a total of four blocks.

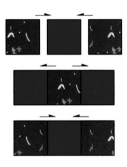
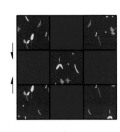

Make 4.

5. Sew border strips from step 3 to the sides of the quilt. Press the seam allowances toward the yellow strips. Add a border corner block to the ends of the remaining two border strips. Press the seam allowances toward the blocks. Sew these strips to the top and bottom of the quilt. Press the seam allowances toward the yellow strips.

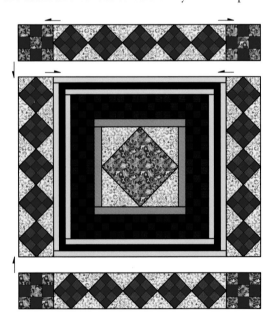

6. From the pieced yellow strip you already made, cut two 2" x 63½" strips and two 2" x 66½" strips. Set the remainder of the pieced strip aside. Sew the 2" x 63½" strips to the sides of the quilt. Press the seam allowances toward the yellow strips. Sew the 2" x 66½" strips to the top and bottom of the quilt. Press the seam allowances toward the yellow strips.

7. Sew the orange 2" x 42" strips together end to end and press the seam allowances open. From the pieced strip, cut two 2" x 66½" strips and two 2" x 69½" strips. Sew the 2" x 66½" strips to the sides of the quilt. Press the seam allowances toward the orange strips. Sew the 2" x 69½" strips to the top and bottom of the quilt. Press the seam allowances toward the orange strips.

8. From the pieced yellow strip, cut two 2" x 69½" strips and two 2" x 72½" strips. Set the remainder of the pieced strip aside. Sew the 2" x 69½" strips to the sides of the quilt. Press the seam allowances toward the orange strips. Sew the 2" x 72½" strips to the top and bottom of the quilt. Press the seam allowances toward the orange strips.

Making the Purple Border Blocks and Frames

1. Sew the dark purple and remaining dark red 2⅝" x 42" strips together as shown to make strip sets E and F. Make the amount indicated for each strip set. Press the seam allowances toward the dark purple strips. Crosscut strip sets E into 64 segments and strip sets F into 32 segments, each 2⅝" wide.

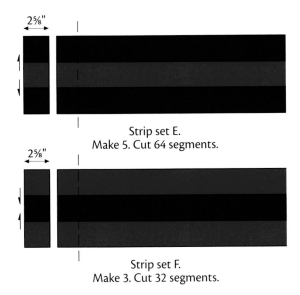

2⅝"

Strip set E.
Make 5. Cut 64 segments.

2⅝"

Strip set F.
Make 3. Cut 32 segments.

2. Sew two E segments and one F segment together as shown to make one block. Press the seam allowances toward the E segments. Repeat to make a total of 32 Nine Patch blocks.

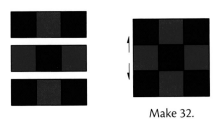

Make 32.

3. Lay out eight Nine Patch blocks, 14 cream multicolored quarter-square triangles, and four cream multicolored half-square triangles in diagonal rows. Sew the blocks and triangles in each row together. Press the seam allowances toward the triangles. Join the rows. Press the seam allowances in one direction. Add the remaining half-square triangles to the corners. Press the seam allowances toward the corner triangles. Repeat to make a total of four borders.

Make 4.

4. To make the border corner blocks, lay out the dark red print and dark purple print 3½" squares in three rows as shown. Sew the squares in each row together. Press the seam allowances toward the dark red print squares. Sew the

rows together. Press the seam allowances toward the outer rows. Repeat to make a total of four blocks.

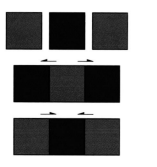 

Make 4.

5. Sew a border strip from step 3 to the sides of the quilt. Press the seam allowances toward the yellow strips. Add a border corner block to the ends of the remaining two border strips. Press the seam allowances toward the blocks. Sew these strips to the top and bottom of the quilt. Press the seam allowances toward the yellow strips.

6. From the remaining pieced yellow strip, cut two 2" x 90½" strips and two 2" x 93½" strips. Sew the 2" x 90½" strips to the sides of the quilt. Press the seam allowances toward the yellow strips. Sew the 2" x 93½" strips to the top and bottom of the quilt. Press the seam allowances toward the yellow strips.

7. From the remaining dark purple pieced strip, cut two 2" x 93½" strips and two 2" x 96½" strips. Sew the 2" x 93½" strips to the sides of the quilt. Press the seam allowances toward the dark purple strips. Sew the 2" x 96½" strips to the top and bottom of the quilt. Press the seam allowances toward the dark purple strips.

8. From the remaining pieced yellow strip, cut two 2" x 96½" strips and two 2" x 99½" strips. Sew the 2" x 96½" strips to opposite sides of the quilt. Press the seam allowances toward the dark purple strips. Sew the yellow 2" x 99½" strips to the top and bottom of the quilt. Press the seam allowances toward the dark purple strips.

Quilt assembly

Adding the Outer Border

Sew the purple floral print 8½" x 99½" strips to the sides of the quilt. Press the seam allowances toward the purple strips. Sew the purple floral print 8½" x 115½" strips to the top and bottom of the quilt. Press the seam allowances toward the purple strips.

Finishing the Quilt

1. Layer your quilt with batting and the pieced backing; baste. Quilt as desired. Quilting in the ditch will be sufficient for the various Nine Patch blocks and frames. However, you may want to consider using an overall or fancier design on top of the checkerboard border. The large center square and the numerous setting triangles in this quilt offer wonderful places to use interesting quilting designs.

2. Trim the edges of the quilt layers even with the quilt top. Use the remaining medium purple 2½" x 42" strips to bind the quilt.

Alternative fabric selections

Some Like It HOT

FINISHED QUILT:
46½" X 61½"

FINISHED BLOCKS:
6" X 9"

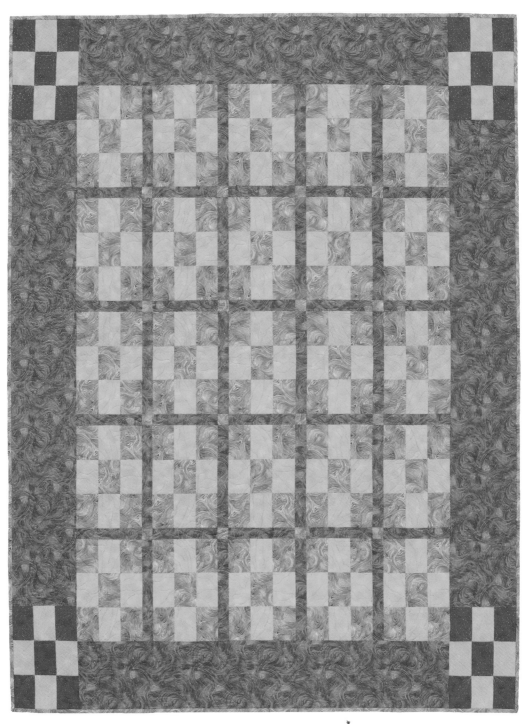

Designed and pieced by Cyndi Hershey. Quilted by Kim Pope.

Swirly prints, hot colors, and metallic accents all combine to show that even a simple design can sizzle! Elongating a typically square Nine Patch block also helps to add personality to this quilt. The color recipe is simple, so feel free to play with fabrics to spice up your own quilt!

Materials

Yardage is based on 42"-wide fabric.

- 1½ yards of light orange swirl print for quilt center blocks, sashing squares, and binding
- 1⅜ yards of dark orange swirl print for sashing and border
- 1⅛ yards of yellow metallic dot print for blocks
- ¼ yard of red metallic dot print for border blocks
- 3 yards of fabric for backing (2 widths pieced crosswise)
- 52" x 67" piece of batting

Cutting

All measurements include ¼"-wide seam allowances.

From the light orange swirl print, cut:

- 19 strips, 2½" x 42"
- 1 strip, 1½" x 42"; crosscut into 16 squares, 1½" x 1½"

From the yellow metallic dot print, cut:

- 13 strips, 2½" x 42"; crosscut 2 strips into 16 rectangles, 2½" x 3½"

From the dark orange swirl print, cut:

- 2 strips, 6½" x 34½", along the *lengthwise* grain
- 2 strips, 6½" x 43½", along the *lengthwise* grain

From the *remainder* of the dark orange swirl print, cut:

- 20 rectangles, 1½" x 9½"
- 20 rectangles, 1½" x 6½"

From the red metallic dot print, cut:

- 2 strips, 2½" x 42"; crosscut into 20 rectangles, 2½" x 3½"

Making the Blocks

1. Sew 13 of the light orange and 11 of the yellow metallic dot 2½" x 42" strips together as shown to make strip sets A and B. Make the amount indicated for each strip set. Press the seam allowances toward the light orange strips. Crosscut strip sets A into 50 segments and strip sets B into 25 segments, each 3½" wide.

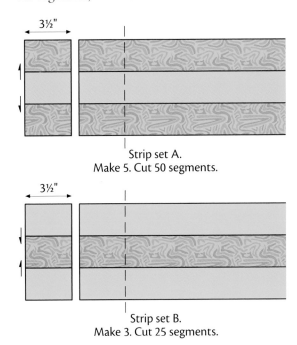

3½"

Strip set A.
Make 5. Cut 50 segments.

3½"

Strip set B.
Make 3. Cut 25 segments.

2. Sew two A segments and one B segment together as shown to make one block. Press the seam allowances toward the A segments. Repeat to make a total of 25 blocks.

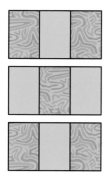 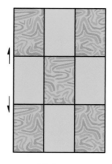

Make 25.

Assembling the Quilt Top

1. To make the block rows, join five blocks and four dark orange 1½" x 9½" rectangles as shown. Press the seam allowances toward the dark orange rectangles. Repeat to make a total of five rows.

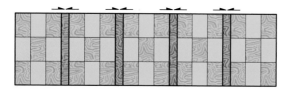

Make 5.

2. To make the sashing rows, join five dark orange 1½" x 6½" rectangles and four light orange 1½" squares as shown. Press the seam allowances toward the dark orange rectangles. Repeat to make a total of four rows.

Make 4.

3. Refer to the quilt assembly diagram at right to sew a sashing row between each of the block rows. Press the seam allowances toward the sashing rows.

Adding the Border

1. To make the border corner blocks, lay out five red and four yellow 2½" x 3½" rectangles in

three rows. Sew the rectangles in each row together. Press the seam allowances toward the red rectangles. Sew the rows together. Press the seam allowances toward the outer rows. Repeat to make a total of four blocks.

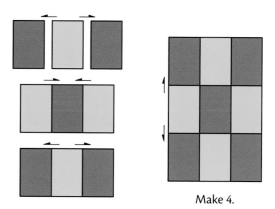

Make 4.

2. Sew the dark orange 6½" x 34½" strips to the top and bottom of the quilt center. Press the seam allowances toward the border strips. Join a border corner block to the ends of the dark orange 6½" x 43½" strips. Press the seam allowances toward the border strips. Sew these strips to the sides of the quilt center. Press the seam allowances toward the border strips.

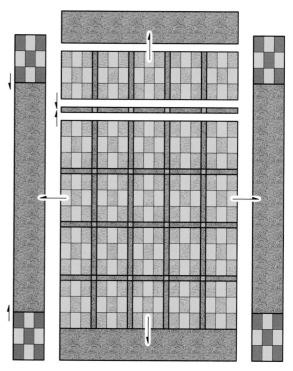

Quilt assembly

Finishing the Quilt

1. Layer your quilt with batting and the pieced backing; baste. Quilt as desired. The sample quilt has elongated sun motifs quilted within each block. Large-scale stippling was used in the borders.

2. Trim the edges of the quilt layers even with the quilt top. Use the remaining light orange 2½" x 42" strips to bind the quilt.

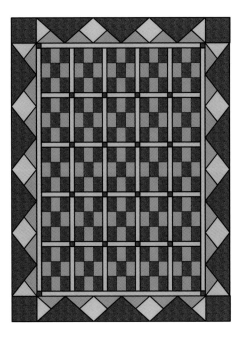

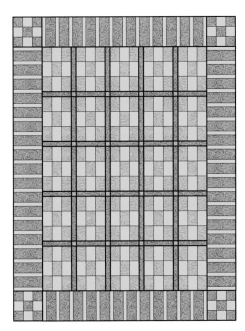

Alternative fabric selections

DIAMONZ

FINISHED QUILT:
48½" X 66½"

FINISHED BLOCKS:
6" X 9"

Designed and pieced by Cyndi Hershey. Quilted by Pat Burns.

If you take a block from "Some Like It Hot" (page 48) and split it in half diagonally, you have the blocks for this quilt! Using strong diagonal lines without any sashing to separate the blocks creates a design that keeps your eyes moving. Select fabrics with minimal pattern for the blocks, such as the tonal batik prints used in the featured quilt, to help increase the overall visual impact.

Materials

Yardage is based on 42"-wide fabric.

- 3½ yards of medium pink print for blocks, outer border, and binding
- 1⅞ yards of light pink print for blocks
- ⅓ yard of yellow print for inner border
- 3¼ yards of fabric for backing (2 widths pieced horizontally)
- 54" x 72" piece of batting

Cutting

All measurements include ¼"-wide seam allowances.

From the medium pink print, cut:

- 23 strips, 2½" x 42"; crosscut *10* strips into 108 rectangles, 2½" x 3½"

From the *remainder* of the medium pink print, cut:

- 2 strips, 5½" x 56½", along the *lengthwise* grain
- 2 strips, 5½" x 48½", along the *lengthwise* grain

From the light pink print, cut:

- 24 strips, 2½" x 42"; crosscut *17* strips into 180 rectangles, 2½" x 3½"

From the yellow print, cut:

- 5 strips, 1½" x 42"

Making the Blocks

1. Use a pencil to lightly draw a diagonal line from corner to corner on the wrong side of 54 light pink 2½" x 3½" rectangles. Repeat with the remaining 54 light pink 2½" x 3½" rectangles, but draw the line in the opposite direction.

Make 54.   Make 54.

2. With right sides together, place a marked light pink rectangle diagonally on top of a medium pink rectangle with the drawn line of the top rectangle connecting the intersecting corners of the bottom rectangle. Sew on the drawn line. Cut ¼" away from the drawn line. Press the seam allowances toward the medium pink print. Repeat to make a total of 108 half-rectangle units.

Make 54.   Make 54.

3. Sew seven medium pink and seven light pink 2½" x 42" strips together as shown to make strip sets. Press the seam allowances toward the light pink strips. Crosscut the strip sets into 72 segments, 3½" wide.

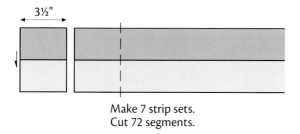

Make 7 strip sets.
Cut 72 segments.

4. Lay out three half-rectangle units, two strip-set segments, and two light pink 2½" x 3½" rectangles in three rows. Join the pieces in each row using *scant* ¼" seam allowances. Press the seam allowances toward the light pink rectangles in each row. Sew the rows together using a *slightly* generous ¼" seam allowance. Press the seam allowances toward the outer rows. Repeat to make a total of 18 blocks of each type.

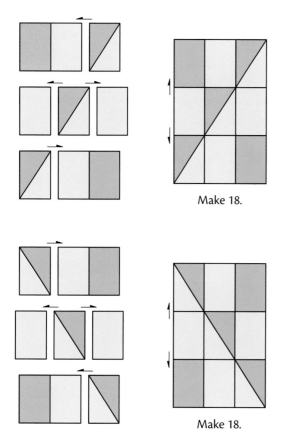

Make 18.

Make 18.

Get the Point

Why use a generous ¼" seam allowance for some seams and a scant ¼" seam allowance for others? It's because the unit shape is a rectangle and not a square. When two ¼" seams intersect at the corner of a square, they meet at the seam point. When two ¼" seams intersect at the corner of a rectangle, they don't meet exactly at the seam point. To compensate for this slight difference, you sew the vertical seams in each row with a scant seam allowance and the horizontal seams that join the rows with a generous seam allowance. This method actually eliminates the need to use templates to cut the triangles for this quilt.

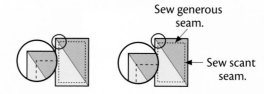

Sew generous seam.

Sew scant seam.

A precise ¼" seam allowance does not intersect the diagonal seam at the corners.

Assembling the Quilt Top

1. Refer to the quilt assembly diagram (page 55) to lay out the blocks in six rows of six blocks each. Sew the blocks in each row together using a scant ¼" seam allowance. Press the seam allowances in opposite directions from row to row.

2. Sew the rows together using a generous ¼" seam allowance. Press the seam allowances in either direction.

Adding the Borders

1. Sew the yellow strips together end to end and press the seam allowances open. From the pieced strip, cut two 1½" x 54½" strips and two 1½" x 38½" strips. Sew the 1½" x 54½" strips to the sides of the quilt center. Press the seam allowances toward the yellow strips. Sew the 1½" x 38½" strips to the top and bottom of the quilt. Press the seam allowances toward the yellow strips.

2. Sew the medium pink 5½" x 56½" strips to the sides of the quilt. Press the seam allowances toward the medium pink strips. Sew the medium pink 5½" x 48½" strips to the top and bottom of the quilt. Press the seam allowances toward the medium pink strips.

Finishing the Quilt

1. Layer your quilt with batting and the pieced backing; baste. Quilt as desired. The sample quilt features a large-scale puzzle design. This simple style of quilting allows for the overall design to be clearly visible without any distraction.

2. Trim the edges of the quilt layers even with the quilt top. Use the remaining medium pink 2½" x 42" strips to bind the quilt.

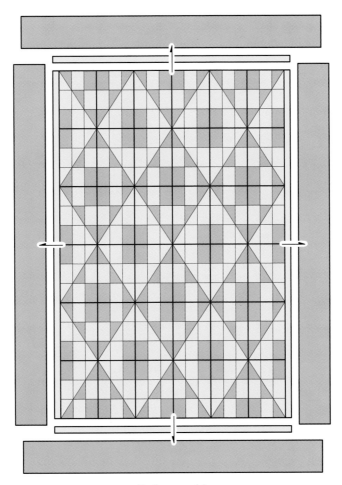

Quilt assembly

Perkiomen Valley NINE PATCH

FINISHED QUILT: 89" X 89"

FINISHED BLOCKS: 8¼" X 8¼"

Designed and pieced by Doris Adomsky. Quilted by Pat Burns.

This traditional quilt design is indigenous to a region of Pennsylvania named the Perkiomen Valley. The majority of the blocks in this quilt are Split Nine Patch blocks. They form the streaks of light and dark fabrics and represent the hills and valleys of the Perkiomen Creek area. The thrifty lifestyle of the Pennsylvania German settlers meant that this was traditionally executed as a scrap quilt.

Materials

Yardage is based on 42"-wide fabric.

- 2⅞ yards of burgundy plaid fabric for border and binding
- 2⅞ yards *total* of assorted dark fabric scraps for blocks
- 2½ yards *total* of assorted light fabric scraps for blocks
- 1½ yards of ivory print for blocks
- 1½ yards of burgundy print for blocks
- 8¼ yards of backing fabric (3 widths pieced in either direction)
- 95" x 95" square of batting

Cutting

All measurements include ¼"-wide seam allowances.

From the ivory print, cut:
- 13 strips, 3⅝" x 42"; crosscut into 138 squares, 3⅝" x 3⅝"

From the burgundy print, cut:
- 13 strips, 3⅝" x 42"; crosscut into 138 squares, 3⅝" x 3⅝"

From the assorted light scraps, cut a *total* of:
- 276 squares, 3¼" x 3¼"

From the assorted dark scraps, cut a *total* of:
- 348 squares, 3¼" x 3¼"

From the burgundy plaid fabric, cut:
- 2 strips, 3½" x 83", along the *lengthwise* grain
- 2 strips, 3½" x 89", along the *lengthwise* grain

Making the Blocks

1. Lightly draw a diagonal line on the wrong side of each ivory print 3⅝" square. Place a marked square, right sides together, on a burgundy 3⅝" square. Sew ¼" from each side of the drawn line. Cut on the line. Press the seam allowances toward the burgundy fabric. Repeat to make a total of 276 half-square-triangle units.

Make 276.

2. Lay out three half-square-triangle units, three light 3¼" squares, and three dark 3¼" squares in three rows. Sew the pieces in each row together. Press the seam allowances in the directions indicated. Join the rows. Press the seam allowances toward the outer rows. Repeat to make a total of 46 Split Nine Patch blocks. Make an additional 46 blocks but press the seam allowances in the opposite directions.

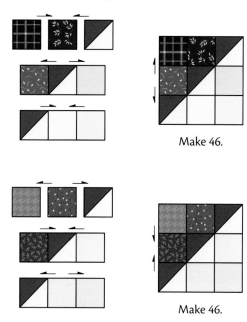

Make 46.

Make 46.

3. Lay out nine dark 3¼" squares in three rows. Sew the squares in each row together. Press the seam allowances in the directions indicated. Sew the rows together. Press the seam allowances toward the center row. Repeat to make a total of eight Nine Patch blocks.

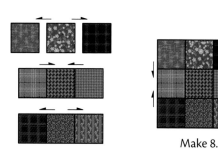

Make 8.

Assembling the Quilt Top

1. Refer to the quilt assembly diagram (page 59) to lay out the blocks in 10 rows. Select the blocks for placement so that the seam allowances face in opposite directions from block to block. This may not work all the time but you should be able to make this work most of the time. You can rotate the eight Nine Patch blocks in any direction to take advantage of the seam directions.

2. Sew the blocks in each row together. Press the seam allowances in alternate directions from row to row. Sew the rows together. Press the seam allowances in either direction.

Adding the Border

Refer to the quilt assembly diagram to sew the burgundy 3½" x 83" strips to the sides of the quilt top. Press the seam allowances toward the border strips. Sew the burgundy 3½" x 89" strips to the top and bottom of the quilt. Press the seam allowances toward the border strips.

Finishing the Quilt

1. Layer your quilt with batting and the pieced backing; baste. Quilt as desired. The sample quilt features a large-scale puzzle design. The gentle curves helped to balance the sharp geometric nature of the quilt pattern.

2. Trim the edges of the quilt layers even with the quilt top.

3. Using the remainder of the burgundy plaid fabric, cut 2½"-wide bias strips. You will need enough strips to equal at least 267" after they are sewn together. To cut bias strips, square up the left edge of the fabric. Working with a single layer of fabric, align the 45° angle of your rotary ruler along the bottom-left edge of the fabric so that it extends completely across the fabric. Cut along the edge of the ruler. Measuring from the cut edge, cut 2½"-wide strips.

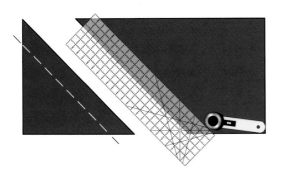

4. Join the strips at right angles and press the seam allowances open.

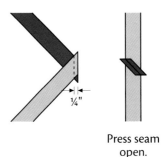

¼"

Press seam open.

5. Use the pieced strip from step 4 to bind the quilt in the same manner as you would straight-cut strips.

Quilt assembly

Winter BLUES

FINISHED QUILT:
53 ¾" X 66 ½"

FINISHED BLOCKS:
9" X 9"

Designed and pieced by Cyndi Hershey. Quilted by Kim Pope.

Combining simple Nine Patch blocks with Double Nine Patch blocks creates a nice balance for this design. The Double Nine Patch blocks form both vertical and horizontal chains throughout the quilt that keep your eye moving. Using a monochromatic color palette as shown in the sample quilt is particularly successful when a variety of values are included in the fabrics.

Materials

Yardage is based on 42"-wide fabric.

- 2½ yards of medium blue print for Nine Patch blocks and outer border
- 1⅔ yards of blue floral print for Double Nine Patch blocks and binding
- ⅞ yard of light blue print for Nine Patch blocks and inner border
- ⅞ yard of dark blue print for Double Nine Patch blocks
- 3½ yards of fabric for backing (2 widths pieced crosswise)
- 60" x 72" piece of batting

Cutting

All measurements include ¼"-wide seam allowances.

From the medium blue print, cut:

- 7 strips, 3½" x 42"

From the *remainder* of the medium blue print, cut:

- 2 strips, 6½" x 54½", along the *lengthwise* grain
- 2 strips, 6½" x 53¾", along the *lengthwise* grain

From the light blue print, cut:

- 5 strips, 3½" x 42"
- 5 strips, 2" x 42"

From the dark blue print, cut:

- 12 strips, 1½" x 42"
- 3 strips, 2⅝" x 42"; crosscut into 31 squares, 2⅝" x 2⅝". Cut each square twice diagonally to yield 124 quarter-square triangles. You will use 122. From the remainder of the strips, cut 2 squares, 1⁹⁄₁₆" x 1⁹⁄₁₆". Cut each square once diagonally to yield 4 half-square triangles.

From the blue floral print, cut:

- 12 strips, 1½" x 42"; crosscut 2 strips into 42 squares, 1½" x 1½"
- 5 strips, 3½" x 42"; crosscut into 48 squares, 3½" x 3½"
- 7 strips, 2½" x 42"

Making the Nine Patch Blocks

1. Sew the medium blue and light blue 3½" x 42" strips together as shown to make strip sets A and B. Make the amount indicated for each strip set. Press the seam allowances toward the medium blue strips. Crosscut strip sets A into 26 segments and strip set B into 11 segments, each 3½" wide.

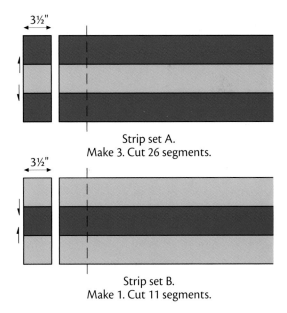

3½"

Strip set A.
Make 3. Cut 26 segments.

3½"

Strip set B.
Make 1. Cut 11 segments.

2. Because you need a total of 12 B segments, you need to create one additional segment. Rather than waste fabric by making another strip set, you will use the two extra segments that you cut from strip sets A. To do this, release the stitching and remove a medium blue square from one

end of one A segment. Release the stitching and separate all the squares from the remaining A segment. Sew the single light blue square to the end of the previous segment and press the seam allowance toward the medium blue square.

3. Sew two A segments and one B segment together as shown to make one block. Press the seam allowances toward the A segments. Repeat to make a total of 12 Nine Patch blocks.

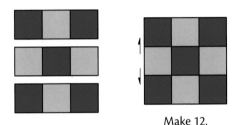

Make 12.

Making the Double Nine Patch Blocks

1. Sew 10 dark blue and 8 blue floral 1½" x 42" strips together as shown to make strip sets C and D. Make the amount indicated for each strip set. Press the seam allowances toward the dark blue strips. Crosscut strip sets C into 80 segments and strip sets D into 40 segments, each 1½" wide.

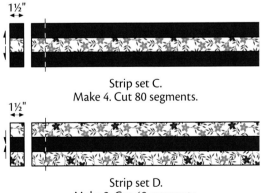

1½"

Strip set C.
Make 4. Cut 80 segments.

1½"

Strip set D.
Make 2. Cut 40 segments.

2. Sew two C segments and one D segment together as shown to make one unit. Press the seam allowances toward the A segments. Repeat to make a total of 40 nine-patch units.

Make 40.

3. Lay out five nine-patch units and four blue floral 3½" squares in three rows. Join the pieces in each row. Press the seam allowances toward the blue floral squares. Sew the rows together. Press the seam allowances toward the middle row. Repeat to make a total of six Double Nine Patch blocks. Set aside the remaining nine-patch units for the setting triangles.

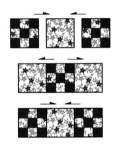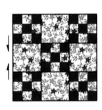

Make 6.

Making the Setting Triangles

1. Sew the remaining two blue floral and dark blue 1½" x 42" strips together as shown to make two strip sets E. Press the seam allowances toward the dark blue strips. Crosscut the strip sets into 38 segments, 1½" wide.

1½"

Strip set E.
Make 2. Cut 38 segments.

2. Lay out one strip-set segment, one blue floral 1½" square, and three dark blue 2⅝" triangles in diagonal rows. Join the pieces in each row. Press the seam allowances toward the dark blue triangles. Sew the rows together. Press the seam allowances toward the outer rows. Repeat to make a total of 38 half-square nine-patch units.

Make 38.

3. Sew dark blue 2⅝" triangles to the sides of a blue floral 1½" square. Press the seam allowances toward the dark blue triangles. Sew a dark blue 1⁹⁄₁₆" triangle to the top edge of the unit. Press the seam allowance toward the dark blue triangle. Repeat to make a total of four quarter-square nine-patch units.

Make 4.

4. To make the side setting triangles, lay out one nine-patch unit you set aside earlier, two blue floral 3½" squares, and three half-square nine-patch units in three horizontal rows. Join the pieces in each row. Press the seam allowance toward the blue floral squares. Sew the rows together. Press the seam allowances toward the middle row. Repeat to make a total of 10 side setting triangles.

Make 10.

5. To make the corner setting triangles, sew half-square nine-patch units to the sides of a blue floral 3½" square. Press the seam allowances toward the blue floral square. Sew a quarter-square nine-patch unit to the bottom edge of the square. Press the seam allowance toward the quarter-square nine-patch unit. Repeat to make a total of four corner setting triangles.

Make 4.

Assembling the Quilt Top

1. Refer to the quilt assembly diagram (page 64) to lay out the blocks and setting triangles in diagonal rows. Sew the pieces in each row together. Press the seam allowances toward the Nine Patch blocks.

2. Sew the rows together. Press the seam allowances away from the center row. Sew the remaining corner setting triangles to the corners of the quilt. Press the seam allowances toward the Nine Patch blocks.

Adding the Borders

1. Sew the light blue 2" x 42" strips together end to end and press the seam allowances open. From the pieced strip, cut two 2" x 51½" strips and two 2" x 41¾" strips. Sew the 2" x 51½" strips to the sides of the quilt center. Press the seam allowances toward the light blue strips. Sew the 2" x 41¾" strips to the top and bottom of the quilt center. Press the seam allowances toward the light blue strips.

2. Sew the medium blue 6½" x 54½" strips to the sides of the quilt. Press the seam allowances toward the medium blue strips. Sew the medium blue 6½" x 53¾" strips to the top and bottom of the quilt. Press the seam allowances toward the medium blue strips.

Finishing the Quilt

1. Layer your quilt with batting and the pieced backing; baste. Quilt as desired. The sample quilt has a very simple curved design quilted in the Double Nine Patch blocks and a straight-line snowflake design quilted in the Nine Patch blocks. The borders contain a swirl design to represent swirling snow!

2. Trim the edges of the quilt layers even with the quilt top. Use the blue floral 2½" x 42" strips to bind the quilt.

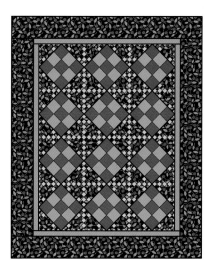

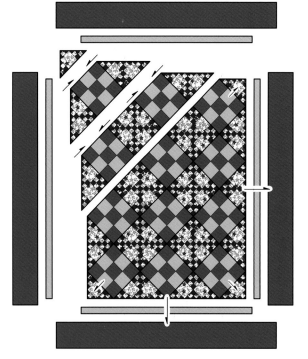

Quilt assembly

Alternative fabric selections

nine by nine by nine

FINISHED
QUILT:
102½" X 102½"

FINISHED
BLOCKS:
27" X 27"

Designed and pieced by Cyndi Hershey. Quilted by Kim Pope.

Here's a quilt that you can finish in no time! These large blocks are perfect to showcase some gorgeous fabrics. Simple Nine Patch blocks are combined with Double Nine Patch blocks, resulting in a strong visual chain that crosses diagonally through the quilt. This would also make a great pattern to use as the top of a duvet cover!

Materials

Yardage is based on 42"-wide fabric.

- 4⅛ yards of peach floral print for blocks and binding
- 3¼ yards of peach floral striped fabric for outer border
- 1¼ yards of yellow print for Double Nine Patch blocks
- 1¼ yards of yellow paisley print for Nine Patch blocks
- 1 yard of green print for Double Nine Patch blocks
- 1 yard of peach print for inner border
- 9½ yards of fabric for backing (3 widths pieced in either direction)
- 108" x 108" square of batting

Cutting

All measurements include ¼"-wide seam allowances.

From the peach floral print, cut:
- 10 strips, 9½" x 42"; crosscut into 40 squares, 9½" x 9½"
- 4 strips, 3½" x 42"
- 11 strips, 2½" x 42"

From the yellow paisley print, cut:
- 4 strips, 9½" x 42"; crosscut into 16 squares, 9½" x 9½"

From the green print, cut:
- 9 strips, 3½" x 42"

From the yellow print, cut:
- 11 strips, 3½" x 42"

From the peach print, cut:
- 9 strips, 3½" x 42"

From the peach floral striped fabric, cut:
- 4 strips, 8" x 108", along the *lengthwise* grain

Making the Blocks

1. To make the Nine Patch blocks, lay out five peach floral and four yellow paisley 9½" squares in three rows. Sew the squares in each row together. Press the seam allowances toward the peach squares. Sew the rows together. Press the seam allowances toward the outer rows. Repeat to make a total of four blocks.

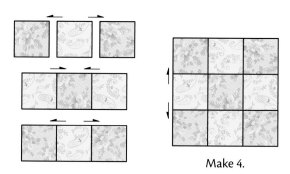

Make 4.

Squares vs. Strips

Why use squares to make these Nine Patch blocks and not strip sets? The strips would need to be cut 27½" wide, which is larger than the length of most rotary mats and rulers. Therefore, it is easier to cut and sew the 9½" squares together.

2. To make the Double Nine Patch blocks, sew the peach floral, green print, and yellow print 3½" x 42" strips together as shown to make strip sets A, B, and C. Make the amount indicated for each strip set. Press the seam allowances in the directions indicated. Crosscut the strip sets into the amount of 3½"-wide segments indicated.

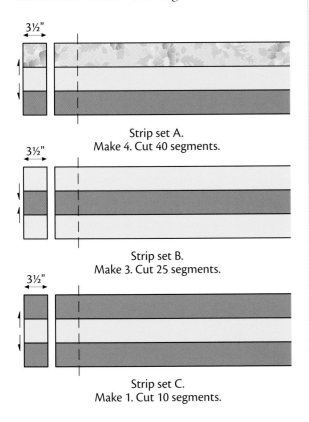

Strip set A.
Make 4. Cut 40 segments.

Strip set B.
Make 3. Cut 25 segments.

Strip set C.
Make 1. Cut 10 segments.

3. Sew two A segments and one B segment together as shown. Press the seam allowances toward the A segments. Repeat to make a total of 20 corner units.

Make 20.

4. Sew two C segments and one B segment together as shown. Press the seam allowances toward the C segments. Repeat to make a total of five center units.

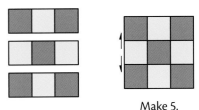

Make 5.

5. Lay out four corner units, one center unit, and four peach floral 9½" squares in three rows. Sew the pieces in each row together. Press the seam allowances toward the peach floral squares. Sew the rows together. Press the seam allowances toward the center row. Repeat to make a total of five blocks.

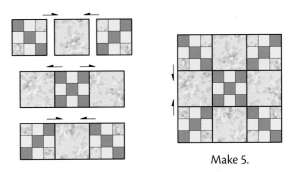

Make 5.

Assembling the Quilt Top

1. Refer to the quilt assembly diagram (page 69) to lay out the blocks in three rows. Sew the blocks in each row together. Press the seam allowances toward the Nine Patch blocks.

2. Sew the rows together. Press the seam allowances toward the center row.

Adding the Borders

1. Sew the peach print 3½" x 42" strips together end to end and press the seam allowances open. From the pieced strip, cut four 3½" x 90" strips. Fold each strip in half crosswise. Pinch the fold to lightly crease it. Repeat to crease the peach striped 8" x 108" strips.

2. With right sides together, pin a peach print strip to a peach floral striped strip, matching the crease marks. Sew the strips together. Press the seam allowance toward the peach striped strip. Repeat to make a total of four pieced borders.

Make 4.

3. Fold the quilt top in half along one edge and pinch the fold to lightly crease it. With right sides together, match the crease marks of a peach print border to the crease mark on the quilt top. Pin the border in place. Sew the border to the quilt edge, beginning and ending a generous ¼" from the raw edges of the quilt top and backstitching at the beginning and end of the seam. Repeat to sew the remaining border strips to the remaining sides of the quilt top.

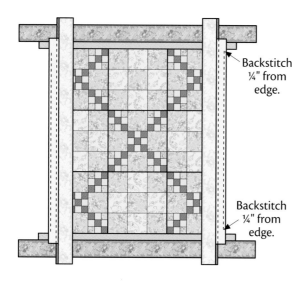

Backstitch ¼" from edge.

Backstitch ¼" from edge.

4. Lay one corner of the quilt on a flat surface. Fold one border strip under at a 45° angle. Use a ruler to check the angle and to be sure that the corner is square. Finger-press or use an iron to press the fold. Use pins to hold the ends of the borders in place.

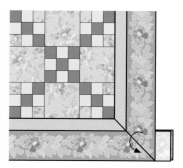

5. Carefully turn down the top border, forming a diagonal fold in the quilt. The raw edges of the two borders should now be aligned, right sides together. Use a few more pins to anchor the layers along the fold line. If you can't easily see the fold line, use a ruler and pencil to draw a line on top of the fold.

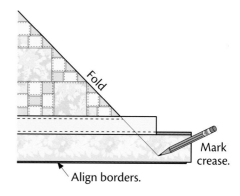

Fold

Mark crease.

Align borders.

6. Sew on the fold line, beginning at the inside corner.

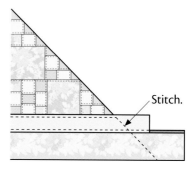

Stitch.

7. Open the quilt and look at the front to be sure that the seam is flat. When you are satisfied that everything looks good, cut away the extra border fabric, leaving a generous ¼" seam allowance.

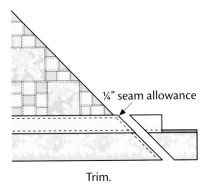

¼" seam allowance

Trim.

Finishing the Quilt

1. Layer your quilt with batting and the pieced backing; baste. Quilt as desired. The sample quilt was quilted with large-scale leaf motifs and vines across the top. The scale of the quilting helps balance the large blocks. There is a lovely continuous vine quilted within the peach inner border that is showcased beautifully against the border fabric.

2. Trim the edges of the quilt layers even with the quilt top. Use the peach floral 2½" x 42" strips to bind the quilt.

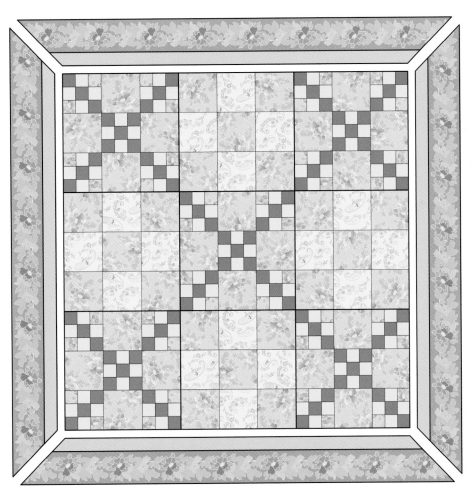

Quilt assembly

Sudoku SAMPLER

FINISHED QUILT: 75½" X 75½"

FINISHED BLOCKS: 18" X 18"

Designed and pieced by Cyndi Hershey. Quilted by Mary Covey.

If you're familiar with the Sudoku puzzle concept then, as a quilter, you may already know that the puzzle is like a Double Nine Patch quilt! In the puzzle, no number (1–9) is repeated within any horizontal or vertical row. In the case of the quilt, each of the nine blocks is made up of nine different units that on their own would be a traditional block. The units are replacing the numbers, so the same concept that applies to the puzzle applies to the quilt design. Feel free to mix up the position of your units as long as you follow the same Sudoku rule! The use of reproduction fabrics in the sample quilt helps give a sense of calm to this visually busy quilt.

Materials

Yardage is based on 42"-wide fabric. Note that in the sample quilt, the background fabric used in each set of nine units is the same, but that each set of units uses a different background fabric. If desired, you can use the same background fabric for all of the units or use a random assortment of fabrics for each set of units. In either case, approximately 3 yards of fabric is needed.

General Materials

- 3 yards of brown floral print for sashing squares, outer border, and binding
- 1 yard of brown vine print for sashing and inner border
- ½ yard of red vine print for sashing and middle border
- 5 yards of fabric for backing (2 widths pieced in either direction)★
- 81" x 81" square of batting
- ★ *Depending on the width of your fabric, 2 widths may be enough to give you the needed width for the backing. If not, you will be able to use the remaining width of the outer-border fabric to add extra width to the pieced backing.*

Friendship-Star Units

- ½ yard of neutral print
- ⅓ yard of gold print

Grecian-Square Units

- ⅜ yard of neutral print
- ⅓ yard of black print
- ¼ yard of grayish green print

Nine-Patch Units

- ⅜ yard of neutral print
- ⅜ yard of dark blue floral print
- ⅛ yard of medium blue print

Double-X Units

- ½ yard of neutral print
- ¼ yard of brown print #1
- ⅛ yard of green print

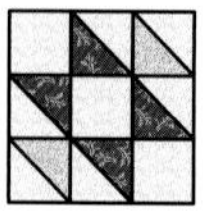

Spool Units

- ⅜ yard of neutral print
- ⅜ yard of blue vine print

Ohio-Star Units

- ⅜ yard of neutral print
- ⅓ yard of dark red print
- ⅛ yard of light red print

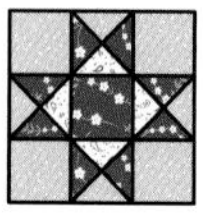

Ribbon-Star Units

- ½ yard of neutral print
- ½ yard of pink print

Rail-Fence Units

- ⅓ yard of neutral print
- ⅓ yard of yellow print

Bow-Tie Units

- ⅓ yard of brown print #2
- ¼ yard of neutral print

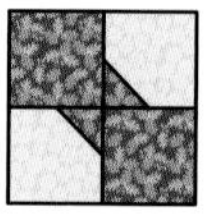

Cutting

All measurements include ¼"-wide seam allowances.

Friendship-Star Units

From the neutral print, cut:

- 3 strips, 2½" x 42"; crosscut into 36 squares, 2½" x 2½"
- 2 strips, 2⅞" x 42"; crosscut into 18 squares, 2⅞" x 2⅞". Cut each square once diagonally to yield 36 half-square triangles.

From the gold print, cut:

- 1 strip, 2½" x 42"; crosscut into 9 squares, 2½" x 2½"
- 2 strips, 2⅞" x 42"; crosscut into 18 squares, 2⅞" x 2⅞". Cut each square once diagonally to yield 36 half-square triangles.

Grecian-Square Units

From the neutral print, cut:

- 3 strips, 1½" x 42"
- 2 strips, 2⅞" x 42"; crosscut into 18 squares, 2⅞" x 2⅞". Cut each square once diagonally to yield 36 half-square triangles.

From the grayish green print, cut:

- 3 strips, 1½" x 42"

From the black print, cut:

- 1 strip, 2½" x 42"; crosscut into 9 squares, 2½" x 2½"
- 2 strips, 2⅞" x 42"; crosscut into 18 squares, 2⅞" x 2⅞". Cut each square once diagonally to yield 36 half-square triangles.

Nine-Patch Units

From the neutral print, cut:

- 4 strips, 2½" x 42"

From the dark blue floral print, cut:

- 4 strips, 2½" x 42"

From the medium blue print, cut:

- 1 strip, 2½" x 42"

Double-X Units

From the neutral print, cut:

- 2 strips, 2½" x 42"; crosscut into 27 squares, 2½" x 2½"
- 3 strips, 2⅞" x 2⅞"; crosscut into 27 squares, 2⅞" x 2⅞". Cut each square once diagonally to yield 54 half-square triangles.

From the green print, cut:

- 1 strip, 2⅞" x 42"; crosscut into 9 squares, 2⅞" x 2⅞". Cut each square once diagonally to yield 18 half-square triangles.

From brown print #1, cut:

- 2 strips, 2⅞" x 42"; crosscut into 18 squares, 2⅞" x 2⅞". Cut each square once diagonally to yield 36 half-square triangles.

Spool Units

From the neutral print, cut:

- 4 strips, 2½" x 42"; crosscut into 54 squares, 2½" x 2½"

From the blue vine print, cut:

- 4 strips, 2½" x 42"; crosscut into:
  18 rectangles, 2½" x 6½"
  9 squares, 2½" x 2½"

Ohio-Star Units

From the neutral print, cut:

- 3 strips, 2½" x 42"; crosscut into 36 squares, 2½" x 2½"
- 1 strip, 3¼" x 42"; crosscut into 9 squares, 3¼" x 3¼". Cut each square twice diagonally to yield 36 quarter-square triangles.

From the dark red print, cut:

- 2 strips, 3¼" x 42"; crosscut into 18 squares, 3¼" x 3¼". Cut each square twice diagonally to yield 72 quarter-square triangles.
- 1 strip, 2½" x 42"; crosscut into 9 squares, 2½" x 2½"

From the light red print, cut:

- 1 strip, 3¼" x 42"; crosscut into 9 squares, 3¼" x 3¼". Cut each square twice diagonally to yield 36 quarter-square triangles.

Ribbon-Star Units

From the neutral print, cut:

- 1 strip, 2⅝" x 42"; crosscut into 9 squares, 2⅝" x 2⅝"
- 4 strips, 2" x 42"; crosscut into 72 squares, 2" x 2"
- 2 strips, 2⅜" x 42"; crosscut into 18 squares, 2⅜" x 2⅜". Cut each square once diagonally to yield 36 half-square triangles.

From the pink print, cut:

- 4 strips, 2" x 42"; crosscut into 36 rectangles, 2" x 3½"
- 3 strips, 2⅜" x 42"; crosscut into 36 squares, 2⅜" x 2⅜". Cut each square once diagonally to yield 72 half-square triangles.

Rail-Fence Units

From the neutral print, cut:

- 6 strips, 1½" x 42"

From the yellow print, cut:

- 6 strips, 1½" x 42"

Bow-Tie Units

From the neutral print, cut:

- 2 strips, 3½" x 42"; crosscut into 18 squares, 3½" x 3½"

From brown print #2, cut:

- 2 strips, 3½" x 42"; crosscut into 18 squares, 3½" x 3½"
- 1 strip, 2" x 42"; crosscut into 18 squares, 2" x 2"

Sashing and Borders

From the brown vine print, cut:

- 12 strips, 1¼" x 42"
- 7 strips, 2½" x 42"

From the red vine print, cut:

- 13 strips, 1" x 42"

From the brown floral print, cut:

- 8 strips, 2½" x 42"

From the *remainder* of the brown floral print, cut:

- 2 strips, 6½" x 63½", along the *lengthwise* grain
- 2 strips, 6½" x 75½", along the *lengthwise* grain
- 4 squares, 2½" x 2½". For the sample quilt, these were fussy cut to feature a small butterfly motif. However, you can simply cut squares and not be concerned about centering a motif if you choose.

Making the Units

Assembly instructions for each of the nine units are detailed below. One of each of these units is included in each of the 18" square blocks.

Friendship-Star Units

1. Sew a neutral 2⅞" triangle to a gold 2⅞" triangle. Press the seam allowance toward the gold triangle. Repeat to make a total of 36 half-square-triangle units.

Make 36.

2. Lay out four half-square-triangle units, four neutral 2½" squares, and one gold 2½" square in three rows. Sew the pieces in each row together. Press the seam allowances toward the neutral and gold squares. Sew the rows together. Press the seam allowance in either direction. Repeat to make a total of nine units.

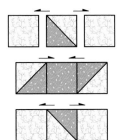 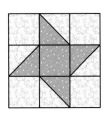

Make 9.

Grecian-Square Units

1. Sew the neutral and grayish green 1½" x 42" strips together as shown to make three of strip set A. Press the seam allowances toward the grayish green strips. Crosscut the strip sets into 36 segments, 2½" wide.

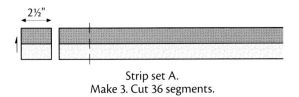

Strip set A.
Make 3. Cut 36 segments.

2. Sew a neutral 2⅞" triangle to a black 2⅞" triangle. Press the seam allowance toward the black triangle. Repeat to make a total of 36 half-square-triangle units.

Make 36.

3. Lay out four strip-set segments, four half-square-triangle units, and one black 2½" square in three rows. Sew the pieces in each row together. Press the seam allowances toward the strip segments. Sew the rows together. Press the seam allowances toward the center row. Repeat to make a total of nine units.

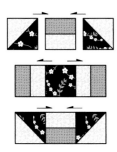 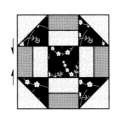

Make 9.

Nine-Patch Units

1. Sew the neutral, dark blue, and medium blue 2½" x 42" strips together as shown to make strip sets B and C. Make the amount indicated for each strip set. Press the seam allowances toward the dark blue and medium blue strips. Crosscut strip sets B into 18 segments and strip set C into nine segments, each 2½" wide.

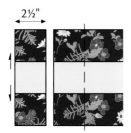

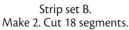

Strip set B.
Make 2. Cut 18 segments.

Strip set C.
Make 1. Cut 9 segments.

2. Sew two B segments and one C segment together as shown to make one unit. Press the seam allowances toward the B segments. Repeat to make a total of nine units.

 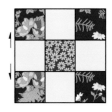

Make 9.

Double-X Units

1. Sew a neutral 2⅞" triangle to each brown #1 and green 2⅞" triangle. Press the seam allowances toward the brown and green triangles. Make the amount of half-square-triangle units indicated for each color combination.

Make 36.   Make 18.

2. Lay out four brown half-square-triangle units, two green half-square-triangle units, and three neutral 2½" squares in three rows. Sew the pieces in each row together. Press the seam allowances as indicated. Sew the rows together. Press the seam allowances in either direction. Repeat to make a total of nine units.

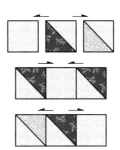 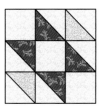

Make 9.

Spool Units

1. Draw a diagonal line on the wrong side of each neutral 2½" square. With right sides together, place a marked square at one end of a blue vine 2½" x 6½" rectangle. Sew on the line. Cut ¼" from the line. Press the seam allowance toward the neutral triangle. Repeat on the opposite end of the rectangle. Repeat to make a total of 18 units.

Make 18.

2. Lay out two units from step 1, one blue vine 2½" square, and two neutral 2½" squares in three rows. Sew the pieces in each row together. Press the seam allowances as indicated. Sew the rows together. Press the seam allowances in either direction. Repeat to make a total of nine units.

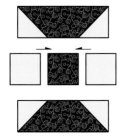

Make 9.

Ohio-Star Units

1. Sew a dark red 3¼" triangle to each neutral and light red 3¼" triangle to make pieced triangles. Press the seam allowances toward the dark red triangles. Sew one pieced triangle of each color combination together. Press the seam allowances toward the light and dark red units. Repeat to make a total of 36 quarter-square-triangle units.

Make 36.

2. Lay out four quarter-square-triangle units, four neutral 2½" squares, and one dark red 2½" square in three rows. Sew the pieces in each row together. Press the seam allowances toward the squares. Sew the rows together. Press the seam allowances in either direction. Repeat to make a total of nine units.

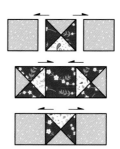
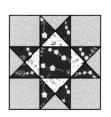

Make 9.

Ribbon-Star Units

1. Draw a diagonal line on the wrong side of each neutral 2" square. With right sides together, place a marked square at one end of a pink 2" x 3½" rectangle. Sew on the drawn line. Cut ¼" from the line. Press the seam allowance toward the neutral triangle. Repeat on the opposite end of the rectangle. Make a total of 36 flying-geese units.

Make 36.

2. Sew a neutral 2⅜" triangle to a pink 2⅜" triangle. Press the seam allowance toward the neutral triangle. Repeat to make a total of 36 half-square-triangle units.

Make 36.

3. Sew pink 2⅜" triangles to opposite sides of a neutral 2⅝" square. Press the seam allowances toward the pink triangles. Repeat on the remaining sides of the square. Make a total of nine center units.

Make 9.

4. Lay out four flying-geese units, four half-square-triangle units, and one center unit in three rows. Sew the units in each row together. Press the seam allowances as indicated. Sew the rows together. Press the seam allowances in either direction. Repeat to make a total of nine units.

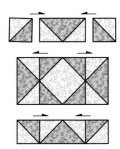 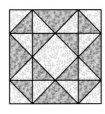

Make 9.

Rail-Fence Units

1. Sew the neutral and yellow 1½" x 42" strips together as shown to make six of strip set D. Press the seam allowances toward the yellow strips. Crosscut the strip sets into 81 segments, 2½" wide.

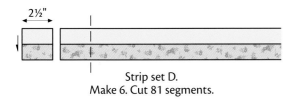

Strip set D.
Make 6. Cut 81 segments.

2. Lay out nine strip-set segments in three rows. Sew the segments in each row together. Press the seam allowances as indicated. Sew the rows together. Press the seam allowances in either direction. Repeat to make a total of nine units.

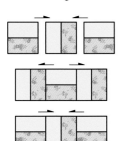 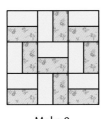

Make 9.

Bow-Tie Units

1. Draw a diagonal line on the wrong side of each brown 2" square. With right sides together, place a marked square in one corner of a neutral 3½" square. Sew on the drawn line. Cut ¼" from the line. Press the seam allowances toward the brown triangle. Repeat to make a total of 18 units.

Make 18.

2. Lay out two units from step 1 and two brown 3½" squares in two rows. Sew the pieces in each row together. Press the seam allowances toward the brown squares. Sew the rows together. Press the seam allowance in either direction. Repeat to make a total of nine units.

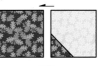

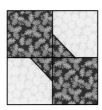

Make 9.

Making the Blocks

Referring to the diagram below, lay out one of each unit in three rows. Sew the units in each row together. Press the seam allowances in opposite directions from row to row. Sew the rows together. Press the seam allowances in either direction. Make a total of nine blocks.

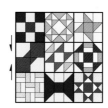

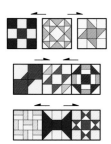

Row 1, Block 1

Row 1, Block 2

Row 1, Block 3

Row 2, Block 1

Row 2, Block 2

Row 2, Block 3

Row 3, Block 1

Row 3, Block 2

Row 3, Block 3

Assembling the Quilt Top

1. Using the brown vine 1¼" x 42" strips and six of the red vine 1" x 42" strips, make six of strip set E. Press the seam allowances toward the brown strips. Crosscut the strip sets into 12 sashing segments, 18½" wide.

18½"

Strip set E.
Make 6. Cut 12 segments.

2. To make the block rows, refer to the quilt assembly diagram (page 79) to lay out the blocks and sashing segments in three rows. Sew the blocks and sashing segments in each row together. Press the seam allowances toward the sashing units.

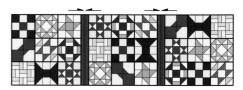

Make 3 rows.

3. To make the sashing rows, sew two brown floral 2½" squares and three sashing segments together. Press the seam allowances toward the sashing segments. Repeat to make two sashing rows.

Make 2.

4. Sew the block rows and sashing rows together. Press the seam allowances toward the sashing rows.

Adding the Borders

1. Sew the brown vine print 2½" x 42" strips together end to end and press the seam allowances open. From the pieced strip, cut two 2½" x 58½" strips and two 2½" x 62½" strips. Sew the 2½" x 58½" strips to the sides of the quilt center. Press the seam allowances toward the border strips. Sew the 2½" x 62½" strips to the top and bottom of the quilt center. Press the seam allowances toward the borders.

2. Sew the remaining red vine 1" x 42" strips together end to end and press the seam allowances open. From the pieced strip, cut two 1" x 62½" strips and two 1" x 63½" strips. Sew the 1" x 62½" strips to the sides of the quilt. Press the seam allowances toward the brown strips. Sew the 1" x 63½" strips to the top and bottom of the quilt. Press the seam allowances toward the brown strips.

3. Sew the brown floral 6½" x 63½" strips to the sides of the quilt. Press the seam allowances toward the brown floral strips. Sew the brown floral 6½" x 75½" strips to the top and bottom of the quilt. Press the seam allowances toward the brown floral strips.

Finishing the Quilt

1. Layer your quilt with batting and the pieced backing; baste. Quilt as desired. The sample quilt was quilted with a large stipple pattern in all of the neutral areas of the blocks. A double row of wavy lines was used to quilt the sashing and a leafy vine was used to quilt the borders.

2. Trim the edges of the quilt layers even with the quilt top. Use the brown floral 2½" x 42" strips to bind the quilt.

Quilt assembly

PICNIC Bouquet

FINISHED QUILT:
42" X 42"

FINISHED BLOCKS:
9" X 9"

Designed, pieced, and quilted by Cyndi Hershey.

This cheery quilt features a variation of the traditional Bouquet block, which is part of the nine-patch category of blocks. In this quilt, the center square has been replaced with a small nine-patch unit. With the blocks set on point, the setting triangles act as a border or frame because they use a fabric that's not used anywhere else in the quilt.

Materials

Yardage is based on 42"-wide fabric.

- ⅔ yard of pink floral print for setting triangles
- ½ yard of ecru vine print for block backgrounds
- ½ yard of ecru plaid fabric for block backgrounds
- ⅓ yard of blue striped fabric for blocks and sashing
- ⅓ yard of pink striped fabric for blocks and sashing
- ⅓ yard of pink daisy print for alternate blocks
- ¼ yard of green plaid fabric for blocks and sashing squares
- ¼ yard of blue dot print for blocks
- ¼ yard of pink dot print for blocks
- ⅛ yard of blue-and-white print for blocks
- ⅛ yard of pink-and-white print for blocks
- ½ yard of blue vine print for binding
- 3 yards of fabric for backing (2 widths pieced in either direction)
- 48" x 48" square of batting

Cutting

All measurements include ¼"-wide seam allowances.

From the ecru plaid fabric, cut:

- 10 strips, 1½" x 42"; crosscut 3 strips in half to yield 6 half strips. Crosscut the remaining 7 strips into:
  36 squares, 1½" x 1½"
  72 rectangles, 1½" x 2½"

From the blue striped fabric, cut:

- 2 strips, 1½" x 42"; crosscut each strip in half to yield 4 half strips. You will use 3 half strips.
- 5 strips, 1¼" x 42"; crosscut into 18 rectangles, 1¼" x 9½"

From the pink striped fabric, cut:

- 2 strips, 1½" x 42"; crosscut each strip in half to yield 4 half strips. You will use 3 half strips.
- 5 strips, 1¼" x 42"; crosscut into 18 rectangles, 1¼" x 9½"

From the blue dot print, cut:

- 3 strips, 1½" x 42"; crosscut into 64 squares, 1½" x 1½"

From the pink dot print, cut:

- 4 strips, 1½" x 42"; crosscut into 80 squares, 1½" x 1½"

From the green plaid fabric, cut:

- 2 strips, 2⅞" x 42"; crosscut into 18 squares, 2⅞" x 2⅞". Cut each square once diagonally to yield 36 half-square triangles. From the remainder of the strip, cut:
  12 squares, 1¼" x 1¼"
  3 squares, 2⁵⁄₁₆" x 2⁵⁄₁₆"; cut each 2⁵⁄₁₆" square twice diagonally to yield 12 quarter-square triangles.

From the blue-and-white print, cut:

- 1 strip, 2⅞" x 42"; crosscut into 8 squares, 2⅞" x 2⅞". Cut each square once diagonally to yield 16 half-square triangles.

From the pink-and-white print, cut:

- 1 strip, 2⅞" x 42"; crosscut into 10 squares, 2⅞" x 2⅞". Cut each square once diagonally to yield 20 half-square triangles.

From the ecru vine print, cut:

- 4 strips, 3½" x 42"; crosscut into 36 squares, 3½" x 3½"

From the pink daisy print, cut:

- 1 strip, 9½" x 42"; crosscut into 4 squares, 9½" x 9½"

From the pink floral print, cut:

- 1 strip, 14" x 42"; crosscut into 2 squares, 14" x 14". Cut each square twice diagonally to yield 8 quarter-square triangles.
- 1 strip, 7¼" x 42"; crosscut into 2 squares, 7¼" x 7¼". Cut each square once diagonally to yield 4 half-square triangles.

From the blue vine print, cut:

- 5 strips, 2½" x 42"

Making the Blocks

1. Sew the blue striped and three of the ecru plaid 1½"-wide half strips together as shown to make one *each* of strip sets A and B. Press the seam allowances toward the blue strips. Crosscut strip set A into eight segments and strip set B into four segments, each 1½" wide.

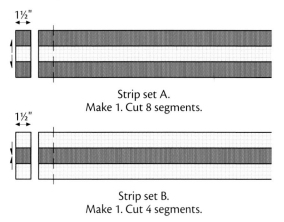

Strip set A.
Make 1. Cut 8 segments.

Strip set B.
Make 1. Cut 4 segments.

2. Sew two A segments and one B segment together as shown to make one blue nine-patch unit. Repeat to make a total of four units.

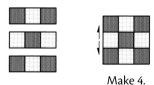

Make 4.

3. Sew the pink striped and remaining ecru plaid 1½"-wide half strips together as shown to make one *each* of strip sets C and D. Press the seam allowances toward the pink strips. Crosscut strip set C into 10 segments and strip set D into 5 segments, each 1½" wide.

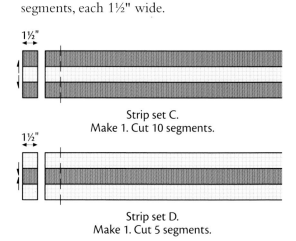

Strip set C.
Make 1. Cut 10 segments.

Strip set D.
Make 1. Cut 5 segments.

4. Sew two C segments and one D segment together as shown to make one pink nine-patch unit. Repeat to make a total of five units.

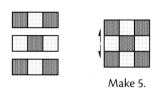

Make 5.

5. Draw a diagonal line on the wrong side of each blue dot 1½" square. With right sides together, place one marked square at one end of an ecru plaid 1½" x 2½" rectangle. Sew on the line. Cut ¼" from the line. Press the seam allowance toward the blue triangle. Repeat on the opposite end of the rectangle. Make a total of 32 blue flying-geese units.

Make 32.

6. Repeat step 5 using the pink dot 1½" squares and the remaining ecru plaid 1½" x 2½" rectangles to make a total of 40 pink flying-geese units.

Make 40.

7. Sew a green plaid 2⅞" triangle to each blue-and-white and pink-and-white 2⅞" triangle to make half-square-triangle units. Press the seam allowances toward the green triangles.

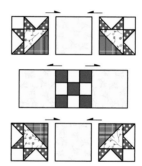

Make 16.   Make 20.

8. Lay out one blue half-square-triangle unit, two blue flying-geese units, and one ecru plaid 1½" square in two rows. Sew the pieces in each row together. Press the seam allowances away from the flying-geese units. Sew the rows together. Repeat to make a total of 16 blue corner units.

Make 16.

9. Repeat step 8 with the pink half-square-triangle units and flying-geese units and the remaining ecru plaid 1½" squares to make a total of 20 pink corner units.

Make 20.

10. Lay out four blue corner units, one blue nine-patch unit, and four ecru vine 3½" squares in three rows. Sew the pieces in each row together. Press the seam allowances toward the ecru squares. Sew the rows together. Press the seam allowances toward the center row. Repeat to make a total of four blue blocks.

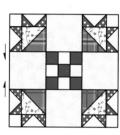

Make 4.

11. Repeat step 10 using the pink corner units, pink nine-patch units, and the remaining ecru 3½" squares to make five pink blocks.

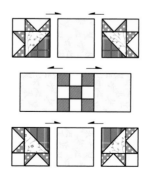 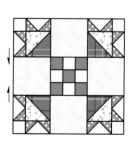

Make 5.

Assembling the Quilt Top

1. Sew a pink striped 1¼" x 9½" rectangle to the sides of each block. Press the seam allowances toward the pink rectangles.

2. Sew the blue striped 1¼" x 9½" rectangles, the green plaid 1¼" squares, and the green plaid 2⁵⁄₁₆" triangles together as shown to make the sashing rows. Make the amount indicated for each row. Press the seam allowances toward the rectangles.

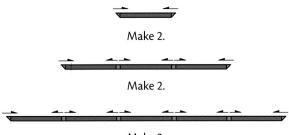

Make 2.

Make 2.

Make 2.

3. Referring to the quilt assembly diagram, lay out the blocks from step 1, the pink daisy 9½" squares, the sashing rows, and the pink floral half-square and quarter-square triangles in diagonal rows. Sew the pieces in each block row together. Press the seam allowances toward the squares and triangles. Sew the block rows and sashing rows together. Press the seam allowances toward the sashing rows. Complete the quilt top by sewing the remaining pink floral half-square triangles to the corners. Press the seam allowances toward the triangles.

Quilt assembly

Finishing the Quilt

1. Layer your quilt with batting and the pieced backing; baste. Quilt as desired. The sample quilt was quilted in the ditch in all of the pieced block and sashing seams. The alternate blocks were quilted with a nine-patch design to repeat the major seam lines of the pieced blocks. The setting triangles were quilted with straight lines of stitching that run parallel to the outer edges of the quilt.

2. Trim the edges of the quilt layers even with the quilt top. Use the blue vine 2½" x 42" strips to bind the quilt.

Nine Patch GARDEN

FINISHED QUILT:
34" X 34"

FINISHED IMPROVED NINE PATCH BLOCKS:
12" X 12"

FINISHED NINE PATCH BORDER BLOCKS:
3 ¾" X 3 ¾"

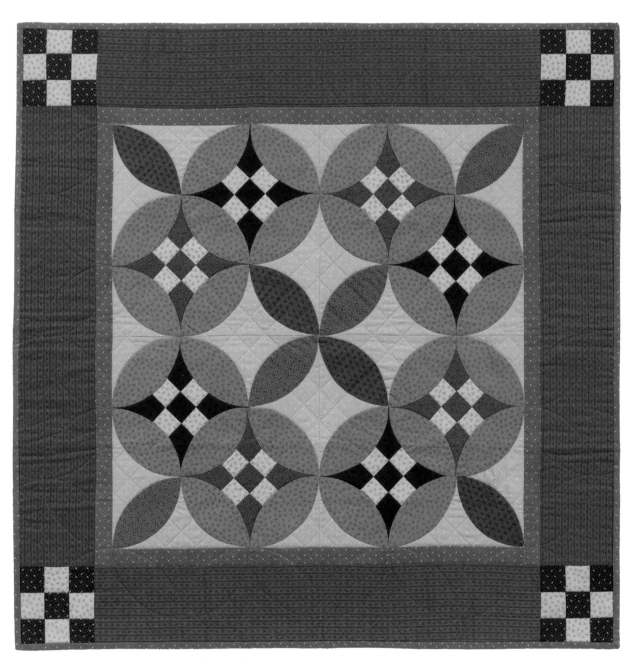

Designed, pieced, and quilted by Cyndi Hershey.

The Improved Nine Patch block is used to create this wall hanging, which uses curved piecing to add interest and visual movement. Using all tonal fabrics helps accentuate the strong graphic appearance of the quilt. This quilt uses templates and is a wonderful challenge for those who are ready to move beyond strip piecing!

Materials

Yardage is based on 42"-wide fabric.

- ⅞ yard of tan print for block backgrounds
- ⅞ yard of red striped fabric for outer border
- ⅝ yard of gold print for blocks
- ⅝ yard of brown print for inner border and binding
- ¼ yard *each* of light tan, purple, and red prints for blocks
- ⅛ yard *each* of teal and olive prints for blocks
- ⅛ yard of blue print for border blocks
- 1⅓ yards of fabric for backing
- 40" x 40" square of batting
- Template plastic

Cutting

Trace the patterns (pages 90–91) onto template plastic and cut them out on the drawn lines. The templates are symmetrical and may be traced onto either the right or wrong side of the appropriate fabrics. Nest the templates closely together when tracing to ensure you have enough fabric. All measurements include ¼"-wide seam allowances.

From the light tan print for blocks, cut:
- 32 template E pieces
- 16 squares, 1¾" x 1¾"

From *both* the red and purple prints, cut:
- 16 template D pieces (32 total)
- 4 squares, 1¾" x 1¾" (8 total)

From the gold print, cut:
- 28 template C pieces

From the tan print for block backgrounds, cut:
- 16 template B pieces
- 8 template A pieces

From *both* the teal and olive prints, cut:
- 4 template C pieces (8 total)

From the brown print, cut:
- 4 strips, 1½" x 42"; crosscut into 2 strips, 1½" x 24½", and 2 strips, 1½" x 26½"
- 4 strips, 2½" x 42"

From the blue print, cut:
- 1 strip, 1¾" x 42"; crosscut into 20 squares, 1¾" x 1¾"

From the red striped fabric, cut:
- 4 strips, 4¼" x 26½", along the *lengthwise* grain

Making the Blocks

1. Lay out four purple D pieces, four light tan E pieces, and one purple 1¾" square in three rows. Sew the pieces in each row together. Press the seam allowances toward the purple pieces. Sew the rows together. Press the seam allowances toward the outer rows. Repeat to make a total of four purple nine-patch units.

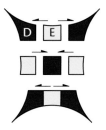 

Make 4.

2. Repeat step 1 using the red D pieces, the remaining light tan E pieces, and the red 1¾" squares to make four red nine-patch units.

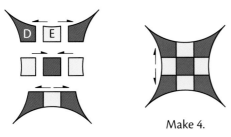

Make 4.

3. Sew gold C pieces to the sides of each purple and red nine-patch unit, sewing with the oval on the bottom and the nine-patch on the top. Stop stitching ¼" from one end of each oval. Press the seam allowances toward the C pieces.

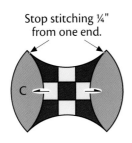

Stop stitching ¼" from one end.

Make 4 purple and 4 red.

4. Sew a gold C piece to the unfinished seam end of a purple unit from step 3, ending ¼" from the end of the seam again. Sew a red unit from step 3 to the opposite side of the C piece in the same manner. Repeat to make a total of four units.

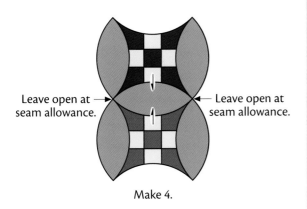

Leave open at seam allowance. ← → Leave open at seam allowance.

Make 4.

Curve Control

Using a single-hole throat plate on my sewing machine gives me more control when piecing, especially when sewing curved seams. Because the hole is only large enough for the needle to pass through, the fabric can't get pulled down with the needle and distort the stitching line. Ask your sewing machine dealer for this accessory if you don't already own one.

5. Sew tan B pieces to each side of the olive and teal C pieces, sewing with the ovals on the bottom. Press the seam allowances toward the ovals. Repeat to make four of each color combination.

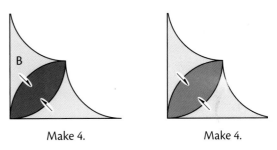

Make 4.   Make 4.

6. Sew a tan A piece to a gold C piece, again placing the ovals on the bottom. Press the seam allowance toward the oval. Repeat to make a total of eight units.

Make 8.

7. Sew matching B/C units to opposite edges of the step 4 units. Begin sewing at the inner point and work toward the outer edge to sew half the seam, then begin at the inner point again and stitch in the opposite direction to complete the seam. Be sure to carefully match seam points at the intersection of the four ovals. Press the seam allowances toward the gold ovals.

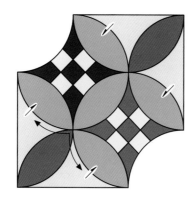

Large arrows indicate stitch direction.

8. Sew A/C units to the remaining sides of the step 4 units to complete the blocks. Press the seam allowances toward the ovals.

Make 2.

Make 2.

Assembling the Quilt Top

1. Refer to the assembly diagram (page 89) to lay out the blocks in two horizontal rows of two blocks each. Sew the blocks in each row together. Press the seam allowances in opposite directions.

2. Sew the rows together. Press the seam allowances in either direction.

Adding the Borders

1. Sew the brown 1½" x 24½" strips to the sides of the quilt center. Press the seam allowances toward the brown strips. Sew the brown 1½" x 26½" strips to the top and bottom of the quilt center. Press the seam allowances toward the brown strips.

2. To make the outer-border corner blocks, lay out five blue and four tan 1¾" squares in three rows. Sew the squares in each row together. Press the seam allowances toward the blue squares. Sew the rows together. Press the seam allowances toward the outer rows. Repeat to make a total of four blocks.

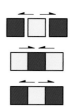

Make 4.

3. Sew two of the red 4¼" x 26½" strips to the sides of the quilt. Press the seam allowances toward the red strips. Join corner blocks to the ends of the remaining two red 4¼" x 26½" strips. Press the seam allowances toward the red strips. Sew the strips to the top and bottom of the quilt. Press the seam allowances toward the red strips.

Quilt assembly

Finishing the Quilt

1. Layer your quilt with batting and backing; baste. Quilt as desired. The sample quilt was quilted in the ditch on all of the block seam lines. The tan background areas were quilted with the same nine-patch design as the block pieced areas. The borders were quilted by continuing the circular shapes formed by the ovals in the blocks.

2. Trim the edges of the quilt layers even with the quilt top. Use the brown 2½" x 42" strips to bind the quilt.

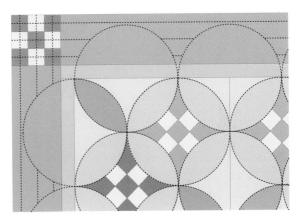

Quilting suggestion

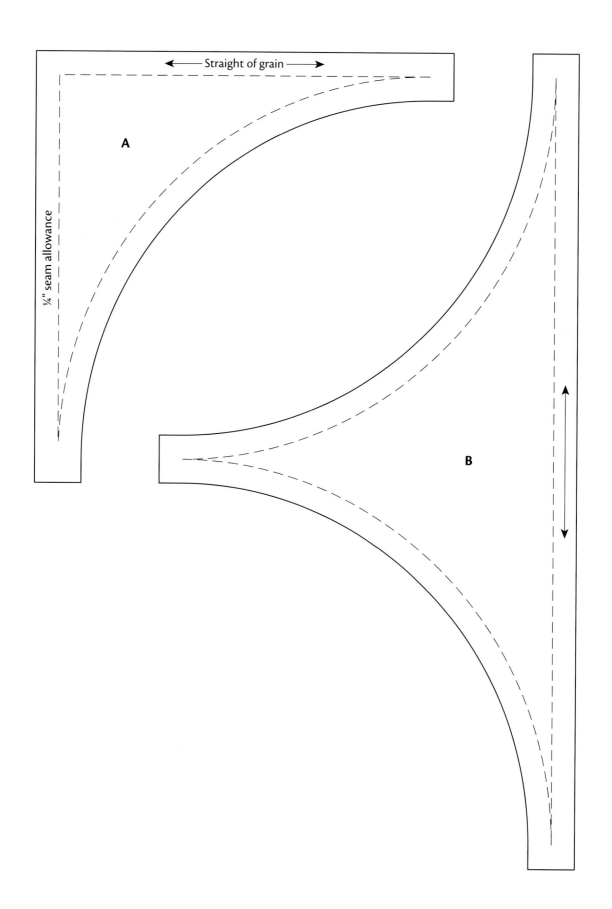

Straight of grain

¼" seam allowance

A

B

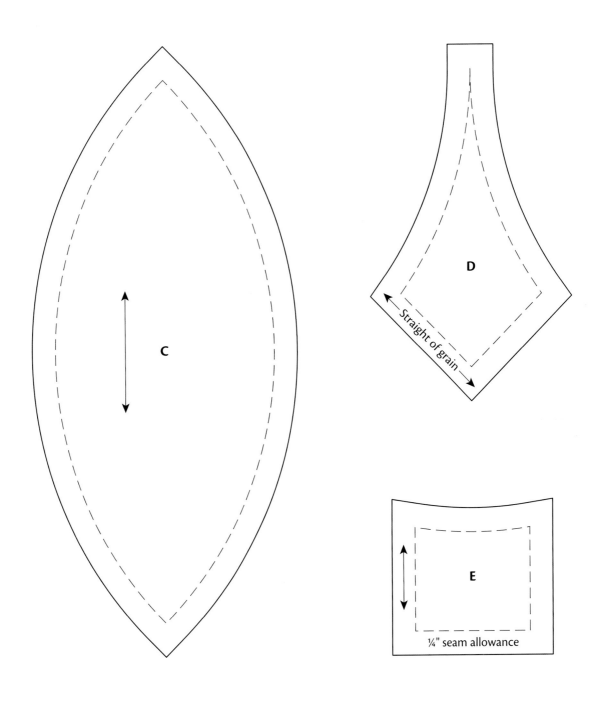

C

D

Straight of grain

E

¼" seam allowance

METRO Runner

FINISHED TABLE RUNNER: 13¼" X 64"

FINISHED BLOCKS: 9" X 9"

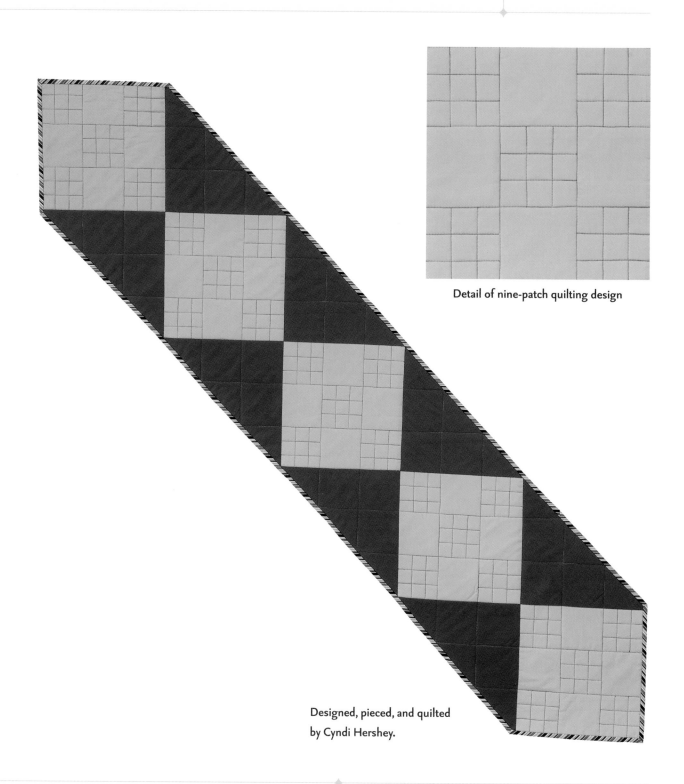

Detail of nine-patch quilting design

Designed, pieced, and quilted by Cyndi Hershey.

Let the quilting be the focus of this contemporary table runner. Solid-colored fabrics are quilted using nine-patch and double-nine-patch patterns. Variegated quilting threads and a striped binding give lots of punch to this simple project. What a great gift idea!

Materials

Yardage is based on 42"-wide fabric.

- 2 yards of brown solid for setting triangles and backing
- ⅝ yard of blue solid for blocks
- ⅜ yard of diagonally striped fabric for binding
- 19" x 70" piece of batting

Cutting

All measurements include ¼"-wide seam allowances.

From the blue solid, cut:

- 2 strips, 9½" x 42"; crosscut into 5 squares, 9½" x 9½"

From the brown solid:

- Cut the fabric in half lengthwise. From one half, cut 2 squares, 15" x 15". Cut each square twice diagonally to yield 8 quarter-square triangles. Use the remaining half for the backing.

From the striped fabric, cut:

- 4 strips, 2½" x 42"

Assembling the Table Runner

1. Lay out the blue 9½" squares and the brown triangles in diagonal rows. Sew the pieces in each row together. The triangles are cut larger than necessary and will extend beyond the edges of the squares. The excess will be trimmed away later. Press the seam allowances toward the triangles. Sew the rows together. Press the seam allowances toward the middle row.

2. Using a fine-point mechanical pencil and a clear ruler, lightly mark a nine-patch design on each blue block. Space the lines 3" apart. Carry these lines into the setting triangles. Mark a smaller nine-patch unit in five of the nine-patch squares as shown.

3. Layer the marked table runner with batting and backing; baste. Hand or machine quilt on the marked lines.

4. Trim the edges of the table-runner layers ¼" beyond the corners of the blocks.

5. Use the striped 2½" x 42" strips to bind the table runner.

Bigger Is Better

Cutting your setting triangles larger than necessary allows for any shifting that may occur in the quilting process. Trimming them to size after the quilting is completed ensures that you will have straight edges and that no points of the quilting design will be distorted.

About the Author

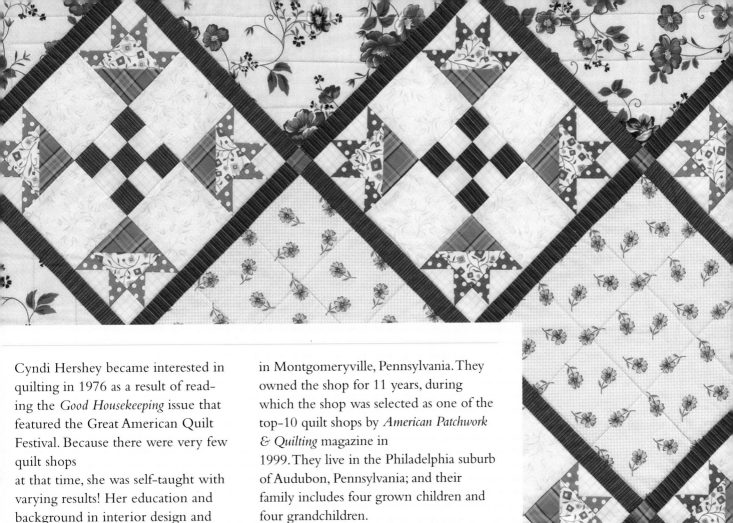

Cyndi Hershey became interested in quilting in 1976 as a result of reading the *Good Housekeeping* issue that featured the Great American Quilt Festival. Because there were very few quilt shops
at that time, she was self-taught with varying results! Her education and background in interior design and textiles were helpful as her interest in quilting grew.

Cyndi began teaching in the early 1980s at quilt shops, as well as at community evening schools. In 1989, Cyndi and her husband, Jim, bought the Country Quilt Shop (now Country Quiltworks) located in Montgomeryville, Pennsylvania. They owned the shop for 11 years, during which the shop was selected as one of the top-10 quilt shops by *American Patchwork & Quilting* magazine in 1999. They live in the Philadelphia suburb of Audubon, Pennsylvania; and their family includes four grown children and four grandchildren.

Cyndi currently works in the art department of South Seas Imports/ Wilmington Prints, as well as for Martingale & Company as a technical editor. She also enjoys teaching others to quilt. See the teacher resource section of Martingale & Company's Web site to contact Cyndi.

NEW and BESTSELLING TITLES from

America's Best-Loved Craft & Hobby Books®
America's Best-Loved Knitting Books®

America's Best-Loved Quilt Books®

APPLIQUÉ
Adoration Quilts
Appliqué at Play
Appliqué Takes Wing
Favorite Quilts from Anka's Treasures
Mimi Dietrich's Baltimore Basics
Sunbonnet Sue and Scottie Too
Tea in the Garden

FOCUS ON WOOL
The Americana Collection—*New!*
Needle Felting
Simply Primitive

GENERAL QUILTMAKING
All Buttoned Up
Bound for Glory
Calendar Kids
Christmas with Artful Offerings—*New!*
Colorful Quilts
Comfort and Joy—*New!*
Creating Your Perfect Quilting Space
Creative Quilt Collection Volume Two
Dazzling Quilts
A Dozen Roses
Fig Tree Quilts—*New!*
Follow-the-Line Quilting Designs
Follow-the-Line Quilting Designs
     Volume Two
A Fresh Look at Seasonal Quilts
Modern Primitive Quilts
Points of View—*New!*
Positively Postcards
Posterize It!
Prairie Children and Their Quilts
Quilt Revival
Quilter's Block-a-Day Calendar
Quilting in the Country
Sensational Sashiko
Simple Traditions
Twice Quilted
Young at Heart Quilts—*New!*

LEARNING TO QUILT
Color for the Terrified Quilter
Happy Endings, Revised Edition
Let's Quilt!
Your First Quilt Book (or it should be!)

PAPER PIECING
300 Paper-Pieced Quilt Blocks
Easy Machine Paper Piecing
Paper-Pieced Mini Quilts—*New!*
Show Me How to Paper Piece
Showstopping Quilts to Foundation Piece
Spellbinding Quilts

PIECING
40 Fabulous Quick-Cut Quilts
Better by the Dozen
Big 'n Easy
Clever Quarters, Too
New Cuts for New Quilts
Over Easy
Sew One and You're Done
Snowball Quilts
Square Deal
Stack a New Deck
Sudoku Quilts
Twosey-Foursey Quilts
Wheel of Mystery Quilts

QUILTS FOR BABIES & CHILDREN
Even More Quilts for Baby
Lickety-Split Quilts for Little Ones—*New!*
The Little Box of Baby Quilts
Quilts for Baby
Sweet and Simple Baby Quilts

SCRAP QUILTS
More Nickel Quilts
Nickel Quilts
Save the Scraps
Simple Strategies for Scrap Quilts
A Treasury of Scrap Quilts

CRAFTS
101 Sparkling Necklaces—*New!*
Bag Boutique
Card Design—*New!*
Creative Embellishments
Greeting Cards Using Digital Photos
It's a Wrap
It's in the Details—*New!*
The Little Box of Beaded Bracelets
     and Earrings
The Little Box of Beaded Necklaces
     and Earrings
Miniature Punchneedle Embroidery
A Passion for Punchneedle
Punchneedle Fun—*New!*
Scrapbooking off the Page…
     and on the Wall
Sculpted Threads

KNITTING & CROCHET
365 Knitting Stitches a Year:
     Perpetual Calendar
A to Z of Knitting
Crocheted Pursenalities
First Crochet
First Knits
Fun and Funky Crochet
Handknit Style II
The Knitter's Book
     of Finishing Techniques
Knitting Circles around Socks—*New!*
Knitting with Gigi
The Little Box of Crochet for Baby
**The Little Box of
     Crocheted Throws—*New!***
The Little Box of Knitted Throws
Modern Classics
More Sensational Knitted Socks
Pursenalities
Silk Knits
Top Down Sweaters
Wrapped in Comfort

Our books are available at bookstores and your favorite craft, fabric, and yarn retailers. If you
don't see the title you're looking for, visit us at **www.martingale-pub.com** or contact us at:

1-800-426-3126

International: 1-425-483-3313 • **Fax:** 1-425-486-7596 • **Email:** info@martingale-pub.com

7/07